Kickoff Foundation

von
David Christie

Ernst Klett Verlag
Stuttgart · Leipzig

Kickoff Foundation

Autor: David Christie, Oxford

Werkübersicht:

Kickoff Foundation Schülerbuch, 978-3-12-808295-0
Kickoff Foundation Workbook mit Lösungsheft, 978-3-12-808303-2
Kickoff Upgrade Schülerbuch, 978-3-12-808296-7
Kickoff Upgrade Workbook mit Lösungsheft, 978-3-12-808304-9
Kickoff Lehrerhandbuch inkl. Digitalem Lehrer-Service mit Medien-DVD-ROM + Lehrer-Audio-CDs (2), 978-3-12-808305-6

1. Auflage   1 7 6 | 24

Alle Drucke dieser Auflage sind unverändert und können im Unterricht nebeneinander verwendet werden. Die letzte Zahl bezeichnet das Jahr des Druckes.

Das Werk und seine Teile sind urheberrechtlich geschützt. Jede Nutzung in anderen als den gesetzlich zugelassenen Fällen bedarf der vorherigen schriftlichen Einwilligung des Verlages. Hinweis § 52 a UrhG: Weder das Werk noch seine Teile dürfen ohne eine solche Einwilligung eingescannt und in ein Netzwerk eingestellt werden. Dies gilt auch für Intranets von Schulen und sonstigen Bildungseinrichtungen. Fotomechanische oder andere Wiedergabeverfahren nur mit Genehmigung des Verlages.

Im Lehrwerk befinden sich ausschließlich fiktive Internet-Adressen, die deshalb auch mit ww#. beginnen anstatt wie üblich mit www.

Die im Buch abgedruckten Mediencodes führen zu interaktiven Zusatzübungen und Downloads auf www.klett.de. Die Mediencodes leiten ausschließlich zu optionalen Unterrichtsmaterialien, sie unterliegen nicht dem staatlichen Zulassungsverfahren.

© Ernst Klett Verlag GmbH, Stuttgart 2014. Alle Rechte vorbehalten. www.klett.de

Redaktion: Gaby Bauer-Negenborn, Weßling; Helen Smyth
Herstellung: Sarah Ganser

Satz und Gestaltung: Marion Köster, Stuttgart
Umschlaggestaltung: KOMA AMOK, Kunstbüro für Gestaltung, Stuttgart
Illustrationen: Uwe Alfer, Waldbreitbach; Tanja Kischel, München; Jeongsook Lee, Heidelberg
Reproduktion: Meyle + Müller Medien-Management, Pforzheim
Druck: PASSAVIA Druckservice GmbH & Co. KG, Passau

Printed in Germany
ISBN 978-3-12-808295-0

Vorwort

Das neue 2-bändige **Kickoff** Bundesausgabe bietet Ihnen praxisorientiertes Englisch für das Berufseinstiegsjahr, die Berufseinstiegsklasse, die Berufsfachschule und die Berufsschule.

— Die Bundesausgabe besteht aus **Kickoff Foundation** und **Kickoff Upgrade**. Der erste Band – **Kickoff Foundation** – führt zum Sprachniveau A2, der zweite Band – **Kickoff Upgrade** – zum Niveau B1.

— Noch übersichtlicher durch das komplett überarbeitete Layout.

— Zahlreiche Differenzierungsmöglichkeiten zur individuellen Förderung durch neue Texte und Aufgaben mit unterschiedlichem Schwierigkeitsgrad (leicht – mittel – schwer) auf den selektiv ansteuerbaren *More please!*-Seiten.

— Zahlreiche inhaltliche Erweiterungen:
  - Viele zusätzliche Texte und Hörverständnisaufgaben.
  - 7 neue Videos zum Training des Seh-/Hörverstehens.
  - 7 neue Doppelseiten *Go for it! The online magazine for students in Germany* zum Abschluss jeder Unit.
  - Alle *Skills* werden mittels *Skills files* ausführlich dargestellt.
  - Berufsspezifische Vertiefung durch *Job pages* im Anhang.

— Vertieftes Vokabular- und Grammatiktraining:
  Kickoff Foundation Workbook
  Kickoff Upgrade Workbook

— Im Preis bereits dabei: neues, interaktives Vokabeltraining online und zahlreiche Downloads durch Eingabe von **Kickoff**-Codes auf www.klett.de.

Am Ende von Unit 4 kann ich:	Lernziele des Lehrplans	V4	Videoverweis
Tips and tricks!	Sprachtipps für deutsche Lerner	→ Grammar	Verweis auf die Grammatik
Hier und dort	Interkulturelles	P, M, I, R	Produktion, Mediation, Interaktion oder Rezeption
→ (Vokabel)	Die wichtigsten Vokabeln auf der Seite auf einen Blick	2se2hk	Vokabeltraining online über www.klett.de und Audio-Download (MP3)
→ More please!	Hinweis auf die Differenzierungsseiten		
Video Lounge	Authentische Videos	△	Differenzierung nach unten
A1.27	Audioverweis	▲	Differenzierung nach oben

| Topics | Language | Check-out activities / Video Lounge / Go for it! |

Entry English, English, everywhere 6

- English as a world language
- introducing myself
- meeting people
- making a phone call
- writing on a social networking site

- *to be*
- pronouns
- possessive adjectives
- genitive *'s*
- *there is/are, to have*
- the time
- simple present statements

- finishing a text and a conversation
- test

Unit 1 At college 20

- talking about myself, my college and my course
- vocational education in the USA
- posting a message on the internet

- simple present statements
- questions
- negatives

- posting messages on the internet
- **Video Lounge:** A stopover in New York
- **Go for it!** How can I improve my English?

Unit 2 People and jobs 32

- naming and describing jobs
- saying why people choose a job
- talking about the present

- simple present with adverbs of frequency
- present continuous

- answering a questionnaire
- making a job profile
- **Video Lounge:** Working as a receptionist
- **Go for it!** Choosing a career

Unit 3 Free time 44

- free time activities
- likes and dislikes
- having a part-time job
- comparing foods, places etc.
- social networking

- verb + -ing
- comparison of adjectives

- doing a class survey
- **Video Lounge:** Go, Greg, go!
- **Go for it!** What is your favourite film, book or TV series?

Unit 4 Products and services 56

- talking and writing about some famous products and services
- talking about the past

- simple past

- collecting and giving information about a product
- mediation
- **Video Lounge:** Making movies
- **Go for it!** Feeling good, looking good

| Topics | Language | Check-out activities / Video Lounge / Go for it! |

Unit 5 Dos and don'ts at work — 68

- talking and writing about workplace rules
- understanding signs in the workplace
- talking and writing about conflict in the workplace

- modal verbs: *must (have to) / mustn't / don't have to*

- talking and writing about the differences between college and work
- **Video Lounge:** Working as a PA
- **Go for it!** What is a good friend?

Unit 6 Success stories — 80

- talking and writing about success stories
- saying how long something has happened

- present perfect with *since* and *for*

- chatting online
- talking about people you know
- **Video Lounge:** Introducing people
- **Go for it!** Who is your hero?

Unit 7 Looking ahead — 92

- talking about one's future
- making plans
- career prospects

- future *will*, *going to*

- doing and talking about a class survey
- **Video Lounge:** Meeting a star
- **Go for it!** Your questions about love

Partner files / Job pages / Test — 104

Partner files   105
Job pages: 106
> Asking for and giving directions
> Getting through on the phone
> Can I take a message?
> Emails at work
Test   114

Anhang Grammar summary / Skills files / Vocabulary — 118

Grammar summary   119
Skills files   128
Grundwortschatz und Zahlen 141
Unitbegleitendes Vokabular 144
Alphabetisches Vokabular   160
Bildquellennachweis   167

Entry
English, English, everywhere

Check-in | Revision | Check-out

1 Hi. Do you speak English?

R **A Read about Silke and Robbie. Where are they?**

This weekend, there's a music festival near Cologne. There are bands from Europe and the USA. Lots of young people are at the festival. Silke and Robbie are there too.

R, P **B Listen. Then read their dialogue with a partner.**

A1.1

Robbie   **Silke**
Hi. Do you speak English?
            A bit!
My name's Robbie.
            Hi. I'm Silke.
Where are you from?
            I'm from Dusseldorf in Germany. What about you?
I'm from London in England.

P **C You're at the festival too. You meet a young woman called Brooke from Chicago, in the USA. Make a dialogue with your partner. Take it in turns to be Brooke.**

Hi. Do you speak English?
...

P **D Say 'hi' to your class.**

Hi. I'm …
Hello. My name's …

P **E Finish the sentences.**

1 Silke and Robbie … at a music festival.
2 Where … the festival? – It … near Cologne.
3 Robbie … English. He … from London.
4 Where … you from? – I … from Germany.

→ Cologne   → lots of   → what about you?   → to meet
→ to take it in turns   → dialogue

Das Verb to be

I am (I'm)	I'm not
he is (he's)	he isn't
she is (she's)	she isn't
it is (it's)	it isn't
we are (we're)	we aren't
you are (you're)	you aren't
they are (they're)	they aren't

Fragen:
Where **is she** from?
Where **are you / they** from?

Am Ende von Entry habe ich:

— die Basis-Grammatik und den Grundwortschatz des Englischen wiederholt,
— Englisch als Weltsprache kennengelernt.

Entry English, English, everywhere

Check-in — **Revision** — Check-out

2 What are their names?

A Lots of people in the world speak English. Where are these native speakers from? How old are they? What are their jobs?

Marianne is from ... She's ... (years old). She's a ...
Phil, Adam and Lilly are ... They're ... They're ...

Hello. Our names are Phil, Adam and Lilly. We're from Britain and we're all 17. We're students.

Hi. My name's Marianne. I'm 18 and I'm from Canada. I'm a secretary.

Hi. I'm Brandon and I'm from the USA. I'm 22 and I'm a construction worker.

G'day. We're Greg and Georgina. We're nurses and we're from Australia. We're 19.

My name's Gordon. Hi. I'm 21 and I'm a computer technician. I'm from New Zealand.

B What are their names? Ask another student.

He's 21 and he's a computer technician.
– His name's Gordon.
She's from Canada.
– Her name's ...

→ secretary   → nurse   → technician

P **C** **Read about Hannah and finish the sentences with the words next to the sentences.**

Hannah is Gordon's girlfriend. Gordon is the guy from New Zealand on the last page. This is Hannah's family.

dad > Patrick
mum > Emma

Hannah and her **sister** Sophie, 19

brother > Jack, 14

1 Hannah's ... name is Jack. Jack is 14.
2 Her ... name is Sophie. Hannah and Sophie are twins.
3 Her ... name is Patrick. He's a painter and decorator.
4 Her ... name is Emma. ... mum is a doctor's receptionist.

dad's
       Hannah's
sister's
       brother's
mum's

I **D** **Ask a partner.**

What's your mum's / dad's name?

Do you have a brother or a sister? What are their names?

R, P **E** **What's right: a or b?**

1 This is Marianne. a) *He's* b) *She's* from Canada.
2 He's from the USA. a) *His* b) *Her* name's Brandon.
3 These two people are from Australia.
   a) *Her* b) *Their* names are Greg and Georgina.
4 a) *Hannahs* b) *Hannah's* dad is called Patrick.
5 a) *Her* b) *His* mum is called Emma.
6 Hannah and Sophie are a) *Jacks* b) *Jack's* sisters.

→ sentence → receptionist

Genitiv 's

Gordon's girlfriend
(Gordons Freundin)

My girlfriend's dad
(Der Vater meiner Freundin)

| Check-in | **Revision** | Check-out

3 A holiday in Montana

R **A Read about Jan.**

1 Where's he from?
2 Where does he want to go this summer?

Jan Wisniewski is from Frankfurt in Germany. Jan likes all sports – walking, cycling, canoeing, football, … This summer, he wants to go on holiday to Montana.

P, R, I

A1.2

B Jan wants to go to a hostel in Montana. You can see the hostel brochure on the next page. Jan is on the phone to Matt, the hostel warden.

1 Complete the sentences below with *there's* or *there are*.
2 Listen and check your answers.
3 Read the dialogue with a partner.

Matt   Jan

High Mountain Hostel. Matt speaking.
　　　　Hi. My name's Jan. I'm from Germany. I have some questions about the hostel. Is that OK?
Sure, Jan. What do you want to know?
　　　　How many rooms are there?
OK. **(1)** *There's* one room for eight people. **(2)** ... two rooms for four people, six rooms for two people and **(3)** ... also four rooms for one person.
　　　　What about facilities?
Well, **(4)** ... a dining room, **(5)** ... four washing machines, and **(6)** ... two computers. **(7)** ... a TV room – oh, yes, and **(8)** ... a small shop.
　　　　Thanks very much, Matt. That's great.
You're welcome. Bye.

───
→ next   → (youth) hostel   → to go on holiday (to)

Welcome to the High Mountain Hostel

ROOMS
- 1 room for 8 people
- 2 rooms for 4 people
- 6 rooms for 2 people
- 4 rooms for 1 person

FACILITIES
- Dining room (breakfast 7.30, lunch 1.00, evening meal 7.00)
- 4 washing machines
- 2 computers with Internet access
- TV room
- Shop (open 8.00 – 4.00 for snacks, drinks, maps etc.)

CONTACT US
- Phone 271-389 24465
- Website www.highmountainhostel.com

C It's summer and Jan is at the hostel. He has some questions for Matt about the town. Take it in turns to be Matt and Jan.

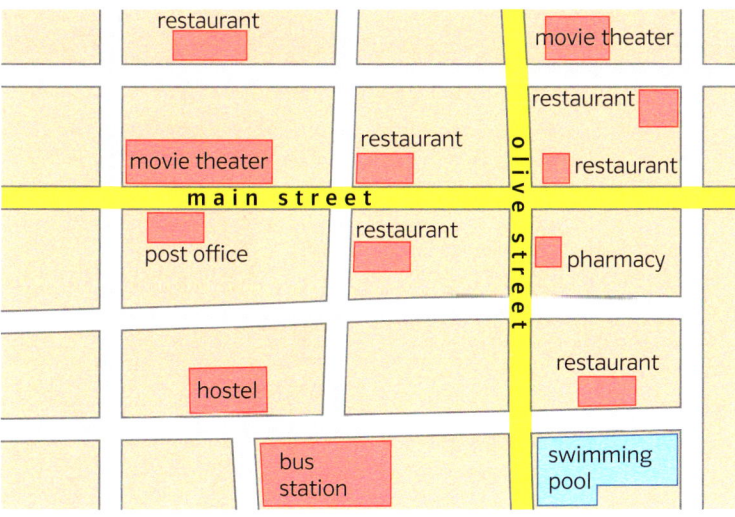

Is there a swimming pool in the town?

Yes. There's a swimming pool here.

Is there a movie theater?

Yes. There are two. Here and here.

→ map   → movie theater (US)   → main street

There's (is) / there are

There's one dining room.
There are two computers.

Check-in | **Revision** | Check-out

4 Rich and famous

A Do you know?

Who are your favourite 'celebs' – famous film stars, sportspeople, singers and musicians – and what do you know about them? Here is a page from a celebrity magazine. Try the quiz!

A QUIZ

MATS HUMMELS

True or false? Write down 'T' or 'F'.

1. Mats Hummels is from Germany.
2. He plays for Germany and Bayern Munich.
3. He is 1.91m tall.
4. He has a younger brother called Erik (also a footballer).
5. He loves computer games – like Wii tennis and playing online games.

LADY GAGA

Which is right? Note down a, b or c.

6. Lady Gaga is from
   a Britain.   b the USA.   c France.
7. Her real name is
   a Maria Gaga.   b Lady Jane.   c Stefani Germanotta.
8. She sings, writes songs and plays
   a the piano.   b the guitar.   c the piano and the guitar.
9. She has 10 tattoos – but where?
   a Only the left side of her body.   b Only on the right side of her body.   c Only on her back.

ROBERT PATTINSON

True or false? Write down 'T' or 'F' again.

10. Robert Pattinson is an actor and was in one of the Harry Potter films.
11. He is from California.
12. He has the middle name 'Jack'.
13. He has an older sister who is in a band.
14. Robert is also a good musician and once played in a band called Bad Girls.

→ musician   → band

R, P, I **B** Ask a student in your class to read out the answers on page 165. How many right answers do you have? Tell the class.

I have … right answers.

P, I **C** What do you have? Work with a partner.

1 First copy and fill in the questionnaire for YOU.
2 Ask your partner the questions and fill in your partner's answers.
3 Tell the class about your partner.
   Linda / Benjamin has …
   (S)he doesn't have …

Which things do you have?	YOU	YOUR PARTNER
1 brothers and / or sisters	?	?
2 a bike / a car / a motor bike / a scooter / a skateboard / inline skates	?	?
3 a laptop / a smartphone	?	?
4 a tattoo	?	?
5 a Lady Gaga album	?	?
6 a poster of a famous person	?	?
7 a musical instrument (a guitar etc.)	?	?

Do you have brothers and sisters?

Yes, I have …

Do you have a …?

No, I don't have …

P **D** Finish the sentences with the correct forms of *to have*.

1 I ... a PC but I ... (not) have a laptop.
2 ... your friend ... a car?
3 He ... a motor bike but he ... (not) have a car.
4 Lots of film stars ... a famous boyfriend or girlfriend.
5 ... you ... a Lady Gaga album? – No way! I think she's terrible!

Das Verb *to have*	
I have	I don't have
he has she has it has	he doesn't have she doesn't have it doesn't have
we have you have they have	we don't have you don't have they don't have

Fragen:
Do I / we / you / they **have**?
Does he / she / it **have**?

→ to fill in (a questionnaire)   → read out   → smartphone

Entry English, English, everywhere **13**

Check-in | Revision | Check-out

5 A social networking site

R **A** Match the clocks and the times.

1 2 3 4 5 6 7

8 9 10

1 ten past four   6 twenty-five to eleven
2 ten to one   7 half past nine
3 five past three   8 (a) quarter to eleven
4 ten o'clock   9 (a) quarter past eleven
5 twenty past six   10 12 o'clock / midday / midnight

I, P **B** Work with a partner. Point to a clock and ask the time.

What time is it? – It's …

R **C** Julie has written about herself on a social networking site.
A1.3 Listen and note down the missing times.

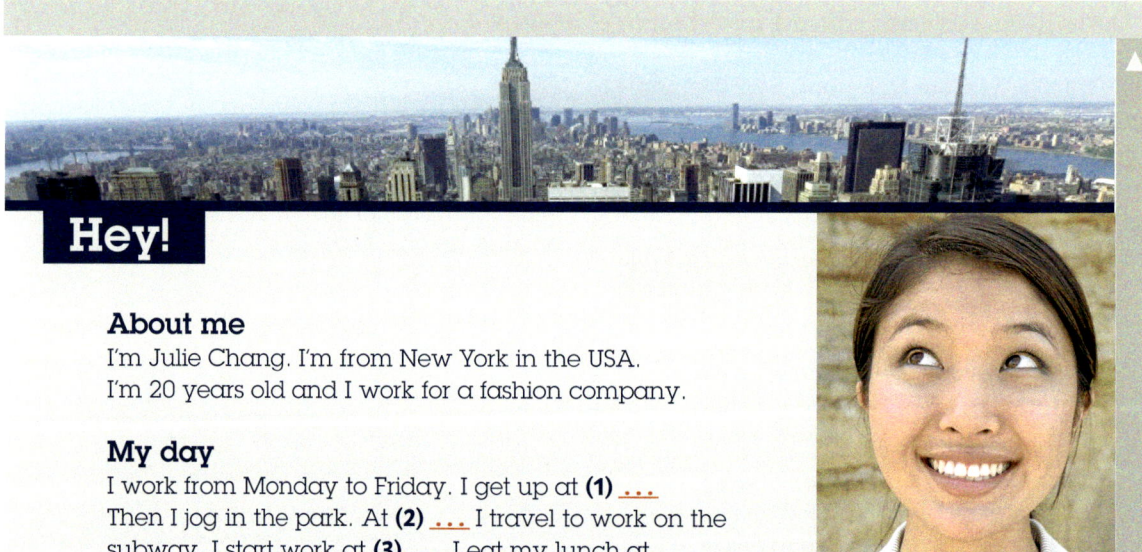

Hey!

About me
I'm Julie Chang. I'm from New York in the USA.
I'm 20 years old and I work for a fashion company.

My day
I work from Monday to Friday. I get up at **(1)** ___
Then I jog in the park. At **(2)** ___ I travel to work on the
subway. I start work at **(3)** ___ I eat my lunch at
(4) ___ I go home at **(5)** ___ I say 'hello' to my friends
in my apartment, then I cook my supper.

→ to match   → to point to   → missing   → social networking site   → fashion   → subway

14

P **D** **Finish the sentences about Julie.**

1. Julie *is* from New York in the USA.
2. She ... 20 years old.
3. She ... for a fashion company.
4. From Monday to Friday, she ... up at 6 o'clock, then she ... in the park.
5. She ... to work on the subway. She ... work at 8.
6. She ... home at 5 o'clock, she ... 'hello' to her friends, then she ... her supper.

> **Tips and tricks**
> Times and days:
> **on** Monday, Tuesday, Wednesday, …
> **in** the morning, the afternoon, the evening
> **at** 6 o'clock / the weekend

R, P **E** **Florian has also written about himself online. Make sentences about him.**

A1.4

He's from …   He's a …   At the weekend he …

Hey!

ABOUT ME My name's Florian Becker. I'm from Duisburg in Germany. I'm 17 and I'm a student at a vocational college.

MY WEEKEND I'm a student from Monday to Friday but at the weekend I'm me! On Saturday, I get up at midday. In the afternoon, I read magazines, I listen to music, or I go online. In the evening I meet my friends and we go to town. On Sunday morning I always go to the swimming pool, then I work out at a fitness club. In the afternoon I meet my friends again. In the evening, we often buy pizza and watch a movie at one of our homes.

P **F** **Now write about YOU.**

- What's your name?
- How old are you?
- Where are you from?
- Are you a student at a vocational college too?
- Write about your weekend.

Das *simple present*

Denk daran: *he / she / it* – das **s** muss mit!

I	work	get	go
he / she / it	work**s**	get**s**	go**es**
we	work	get	go
you	work	get	go
they	work	get	go

→ vocational college

Check-in · Revision · Check-out

6 What can you understand?

R, P **A Look at the pictures. Find ...**

a waiter · a bus driver · a girl in a shoe shop · a hotel receptionist ·
a shop assistant · a mechanic · a man in a restaurant ·
a backpacker · a woman with a car

A

B

E

C

D

R **B Listen to these five short conversations. Match the pictures and the conversations.**

A 1.5

Conversation 1:   *That's picture ...*

R, P **C Listen again. What can you understand? Make sentences.**

1	The man in the restaurant wants ...
2	The backpacker on the bus wants ...
3	The woman with the mechanic has ...
4	The man on the phone to the hotel wants ...
5	The girl in the shoe shop wants ...

A	to go to the youth hostel.
B	to know her shoe size in Germany.
C	to know about 'Gemüse'.
D	a problem with her car.
E	to book a room.

→ conversation   → to want to (go)   → on the phone

Hier und dort
Do you speak English?
Englisch hat sich zu einer echten Weltsprache entwickelt. Man begegnet ihr überall: in Liedern, mit native speakers auf einem Musikfest, auf Reisen, im Internet oder in der Arbeit mit ausländischen Kunden.
— In *Entry* hast du verschiedene Personen kennengelernt, die Englisch sprechen. Kennst du weitere Personen oder Situationen? Gib Beispiele.
— „Wenn Engländer oder Amerikaner in Deutschland Urlaub machen, sollten sie Deutsch können!" Findest du das auch?

16

7 Check-out

A Paul is a hotel receptionist at a hotel in London. Finish the text with the verbs on the right.

Hey!
My name's Paul Everest and **(1)** *I'm* from England. I'm 21 years old and I **(2)** ... in London, England's capital city. I'm a hotel receptionist.

>>>> **My family** >>>>>>>>>>>>>>>>>>>>>>>>>>>>>>>>>>>>>
My dad's name is John. He also **(3)** ... in a hotel. **(4)** ... a restaurant manager. My mum is a shop assistant. I **(5)** ... two younger brothers and one older sister. My two brothers **(6)** ... students at a vocational college in London. Gary (the youngest) **(7)** ... to be a mechanic and Jason a restaurant cook. My sister Jacqui **(8)** ... and she **(9)** ... two children. She **(10)** ... in the north of England.

>>>> **My job** >>
My hotel **(11)** ... the Heathrow Crown Hotel. There **(12)** ... about 250 rooms. There **(13)** ... also a restaurant. It is near London airport and we **(14)** ... always busy. From Monday to Friday I **(15)** ... work at 2 o'clock in the afternoon and I **(16)** ... at 10 o'clock in the evening. When I'm at work, I **(17)** ... the telephone, **(18)** ... rooms and welcome guests when they arrive at the hotel. I like my job very much. I **(19)** ... lots of interesting people from around the world.

>>>> **Free time!** >>>>>>>>>>>>>>>>>>>>>>>>>>>>>>>>>>>>
In my free time I jog, read, **(20)** ... to music and **(21)** ... the internet. I also **(22)** ... to a fitness club twice a week. But the best thing for me is my friends. At the weekends we usually **(23)** ... on the underground into the city. I **(24)** ... living in London. There **(25)** ... always so many interesting things to do.

answer
are (4 x)   book
   finish   go
has   have
   He's   I'm
         is
is called
      is married
   listen
            live
lives   love
   meet   start
surf
      travel
wants   works

B Write a short text about Paul's free time. Look at the last part of the text. Begin like this:

In his free time Paul …

Entry English, English, everywhere   **17**

Check-in | Revision | **Check-out**

P **C EXTRA** Imagine you are one of Paul's brothers or his sister. Write about yourself.

P **D** Paul is speaking on the phone to a guest. Finish the conversation with words and phrases on the right.

Paul	Guest
Good morning. Heathrow Crown Hotel. Paul **(1)**	
	Hi. **(2)** .... a room for this evening, please.
Is that a single room or a double room?	
	A **(3)** .... , please.
I'm very sorry, sir. I **(4)** .... a single room this evening. But you can have a double room. It only costs another £10.	
	That's fine, thanks.
Can I take your **(5)** .... , please?	
	Yes, It's Kowalski, Scott Kowalski. I'm from Chicago, USA.
OK, Mr Kowalski. That's all booked.	
	(6) ....
(7) .... . **(8)**	
	Bye now.

Bye
don't have
I'd like to book
name
single
speaking
Thanks very much
You're welcome

R **E** Write the times in words. There are three answers for one of the clocks!

A B C D E F

P **F** Janine is an American college student. This is a picture of her with her friends. Finish the sentences. Use *my*, *your*, *his*, *her*, *our* and *their*.

1 "Hi! *My* name's Janine. I'm a college student in the U.S."
2 Person A is one of Janine's friends. .... name is Bruce.
3 Next to Bruce is another friend. .... name is Julie-Ann.
4 The two people, C, are two more friends. .... names are Trudi and Don.
5 "Hi! We're the C people! .... names are Trudi and Don."
6 "And I'm person D. .... name's Max.
7 And you. What's .... name?

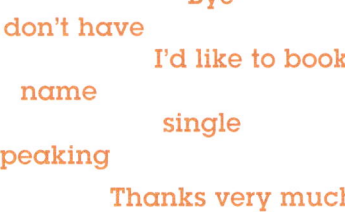

Janine   A   B   C+C   D

18

G TEST YOURSELF What can you do now? Find out! Choose the correct answer a, b or c.

Question		a	b	c
1	My name's Charlotte. What's ... name? – I'm Christoph.	my	her	your
2	Where ... you from? – I'm from Germany.	are	is	am
3	This is my friend. ... name's Anja.	Their	Her	Our
4	My ... name is John.	brothers'	brothers	brother's
5	... three rooms at the hostel for two people.	There's	There are	Is there
6	How many computers are there? – ... one.	There's	There are	Is there
7	... smartphone? – Yes, and a laptop.	Have you	Does you have	Do you have
8	Mike has a PC but he ... have a laptop.	don't have	doesn't have	has not
9	Lots of people in my class ... a bike.	have	are have	is have
10	What time is it? – It's 3.30.	= half past four	= half past three	= half to four
11	What time is it now? – It's 6.45.	= a quarter past six	= a quarter before six	= a quarter to seven
12	Hi. My name's Mary-Lou and I ... in New York.	works	am work	work
13	At the weekend, Oliver ... up at midday.	is get	get	gets
14	Jack and his two friends often ... to the cinema at the weekend.	go	goes	are go
15	I'm from England. ... about you?	Where	What	From
16	Greg is from ...	australia.	Australien.	Australia.
17	Tony eats his lunch ... 1 o'clock.	on	at	in
18	I watch TV ... the evening.	on	at	in
19	White Horse Hotel. Nicole ...	speak.	speaking.	speaks.
20	Thanks very much. – You're ...	OK.	welcome.	goodbye.

CollegeNet

The International Network of Vocational Colleges

FIND A PARTNER >> search >> post a message

Here you can
- find partner colleges in more than 20 countries worldwide
- use the website as a platform to get to know students like you around the world
- organise projects between colleges
- organise international visits and exchanges

Country USA
College Kansas West Community College

Hey!
We are students in a class at KWCC (Kansas West Community College) in Kansas City, Kansas, USA. We would like to get to know students like us who are training for jobs at a college in another country. We would particularly like to hear from students from Europe. Interested? Leave us a message and we'll get back to you. Hoping to hear from you soon!

Unit 1
At college

Check-in | Training | More please! | Check-out

1 CollegeNet

R, I, P **A** Look at the picture on the left and answer these questions. Compare your answers with a partner, then tell the class.

1. How many people are there in the picture?
   There are …
2. How many boys are there and how many girls?
3. Where are they? At home? At college? In town? …?
4. What do you think? What country are they from?
   We think …

> **Hier und dort**
>
> Sowohl in den USA als auch in Großbritannien und in einigen anderen englischsprachigen Ländern findet die Berufsbildung auf einem **college** statt, und die Lernenden sind **students**. In **Kickoff** benutzen wir durchgehend diese Wörter für dich und deine Schule.

R, P **B** Read the web page and the message on the left.

1. What city, country and college are the students from on page 20?
2. What is the name of the website where you can read their message?
3. Say something in your own words about the website (who is it for? what can you do on the site?)
4. What would these students 'particularly' like to do?
5. What must you do if you want to get to know these students better?

M **C** Find the words and phrases in the students' message.

„Wir werden uns wieder bei euch melden."

„Hallo!"

„Wir hoffen bald von euch zu hören!"

> **Am Ende von Unit 1 kann ich:**
> — über mich, meine Schule und meinen Kurs reden
> — etwas von der beruflichen Erziehung in den USA erzählen
> — eine Mitteilung ins Netz stellen.

→ community college (US)   → to leave a message

Unit 1 At college

Check-in | **Training** | More please! | Check-out

2 Meet Clyde and Beth

R, P
A1.6

A Read what Clyde says, then finish the sentences about him below.

Hi again. I'm Clyde. I'm 18 years old and I live in Kansas City, Kansas. I'm a student at KWCC, the Kansas West Community College. I'm on a business course, and when I finish the course, I want to work in a marketing company, maybe in Kansas City.

My course is full-time. I go to college five days a week from Monday to Friday. Most days, the lessons start at 8.30 in the morning and finish at around 2.30 in the afternoon. We get a lunch break from twelve to one. There are lots of sports clubs at KWCC and in the afternoons I usually play basketball or do athletics.

There are 20 people in my class. They're all great guys and I often hang out with them at the weekend.

1 Clyde *lives* in Kansas City.
2 He's on a business course and when he ... the course, he ... maybe to work in a marketing company.
3 Clyde ... to college five days a week.
4 Most days his lessons ... at 8.30. He ... a lunch break from twelve to one.
5 In the afternoons he usually ... basketball or he ... athletics.
6 He thinks the people in his class are OK. He often ... out with them at the weekend.

P **B** What about YOU? Make sentences with the phrases on the right.

"I'm … years old."

"I'm a student at …"

"I go to college … days a week"

"My lessons …"

"I live …"

P **C** Can you give the missing forms?

The simple present				→ More please **A – C**
	want	live	go	finish
I	?	live	go	finish
he / she / it	wants	?	goes	finishes
we	want	live	?	finish
you	want	live	go	?
they	want	live	?	finish

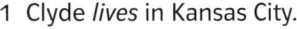
→ to be on a course   → most days   → to do athletics

Tips and tricks
Nicht vergessen:
he / she / it das *s* muss mit!

 D Now listen to Beth. Which is right? Note down a) or b).
A 1.7

1 Beth is   a) 18 years old   b) 19 years old.
2 She's in the   a) first   b) second year of her course.
3 She   a) knows   b) doesn't know what job she wants to have after college.
4 Her father   a) works in an office   b) is a truck driver.
5 She   a) has   b) doesn't have four brothers and sisters.
6 Kansas City   a) is   b) isn't in just one state.
7 The city has   a) 500,000   b) 750,000 people.
8 Beth   a) likes   b) doesn't like Kansas City.

R, P **E What's the same and what's different for YOU? Copy and fill in the table below then make sentences.**

Beth is 18 but I'm not 18. I'm …

	Beth	Me
age	18	?
knows what job she wants?	?	?
family	?	?
likes where she lives?	?	?

P **F Can you give the missing forms?**

Das simple present: Verneinung		→ More please **D, E**
I	?	
he / she / it	?	live in California.
we / you / they	don't	

→ to finish sth   → truck driver   → kinda (US slang) = kind of

Unit 1 At college   23

Check-in — **Training** — More please! — Check-out

3 A brochure

R **A Read about Amber.**

Amber Johnson is a student at Oaklands High School in Kansas City. Almost all American teenagers go to high school and they leave when they're 18 years old. Amber is 18 now, so it's her last year at school. Next year she wants to go to KWCC. She wants to be a computer technician. Today, she has a brochure about the college. You can see a page from the brochure on page 25.

1 Where does she go to high school? How old is she?
2 What does she want to do next year?
3 What job does Amber want to have one day?

R **B Amber has lots of questions about the college and the courses there. Look at the brochure and find the answers for her.** → Skills 1

1 How big is the college and how many students are there?
2 How many courses does the college offer?
3 Can I train to be a computer technician?
4 How long do the courses last?
5 How much do the courses cost?
6 How can I contact the college?

P **C What about YOU?**

1 Where is your college? Does your college have a name?
2 How long does your course last?
3 How much does your course cost?

R **D Can you give the missing forms?**

Das simple present: Fragen			→ More please! **F – H**
	do	I	
Where	?	he / she / it	live?
	?	we / you / they	

→ to want to (do sth)   → a brochure   → to last (one year / two years)   → to cost

KANSAS WEST COMMUNITY COLLEGE

WHO DO YOU WANT TO BE?

With over 8,000 students, KWCC is one of the biggest community colleges in Kansas. Most students come to us after high school at 18, but the college is for everyone. Our oldest student at the moment is 75!

Because we are so big, we offer over 200 different courses. So whether you want to be a hairdresser or a secretary, a computer technician or a dancer, we can help you.

Courses at KWCC don't last 'a year' or 'two years'. You get 'credits' when you come to classes. When you have enough credits, you finish the course. So you can finish your course in one year, two years, or even longer if you want.

Courses cost between $1,000 and $5,000 dollars but you can get help with money if you need it. We have all the details – just come and talk to us.

COURSES AT KWCC

We offer courses in all these subject areas …

> Art and Design
> Automotive Mechanics
> Business and Business Administration
> Computers and Information Technology
> Construction
> Health and Beauty
> Music and Media
> Retail Services
> Social Work and Child Care
> Sport
> Electronics

How to contact us:

Visit our website:
www.kwcc.edu

Email us at:
info@kwcc.edu

Call us on:
913 318-40 05 (toll free)

→ at the moment → enough → it costs ($1,000 dollars)

Check-in | Training | **More please!** | Check-out

4 More please!

A Das simple present → Grammar 1

Here are some more sentences about Clyde. Choose the correct forms of the verbs. Write out the correct sentences in full.

1 Clyde **lives** in the USA.
  a live   b lives   c livs
2 He .... to work in a marketing company after college.
  a want   b wants   c wantes
3 He .... to college every day from Monday to Friday.
  a go   b gos   c goes
4 He .... a lunch break from 12 o'clock to 1 o'clock.
  a gets   b get   c getes
5 In the afternoons after his classes he often .... basketball.
  a plays   b play   c playes
6 He also often .... athletics.
  a do   b dos   c does
7 He .... the other people in his class and often .... out with them.
  a like / hangs   b likes / hang   c likes / hangs

I often hang out with my friends at the weekend.

B Das simple present → Grammar 1

Finish these sentences about YOU in your own words.

1 Hi! My name .... (to be) .... (your name).
2 I .... (to live) in .... (town) in Germany and I .... (to be) .... (number) years old.
3 I .... (to go) to a vocational college in .... (town). It .... (to be) called ... (name of college).
4 My lessons usually .... (to start) at .... (time) and they normally .... (to finish) at .... (time).
5 There .... (to be) .... (number) people in my class today.
6 When I'm not at college, I often .... (to go to town? to play ... ? to do ...? to hang out with ...? ...?)

C Das simple present → Grammar 1

Finish the text about Ray with the correct forms of the verbs on the right. You can use some of the verbs more than once. Then imagine you are Ray. Write a short text about yourself.

Ray **(1)** *is* a student at KWCC. He **(2)** .... on a business course at the college and when he **(3)** .... the course he **(4)** .... to travel and to work in Europe – maybe in Germany. Ray's family came from Germany and he **(5)** .... an uncle there. His uncle **(6)** .... in Cologne. Ray **(7)** .... to college five days a week. His lessons normally **(8)** .... at 8.30 and they **(9)** .... at 2.30. KWCC **(10)** .... its own radio station and in the afternoons Ray often **(11)** .... in the studio: he is good with technical things. Ray really **(12)** .... the other people in his class. He **(13)** .... that they are friendly and open. Ray and the other students often **(14)** .... together at the weekend. They **(15)** .... to the mall in the city centre or, in the summer, to the park.

to be
to finish
to go
to hang out
to have
to like
to live
to start
to think
to want
to work

D Das simple present: Verneinung → Grammar 1

All the information about Beth below is false! Correct the information like this:

No! Beth doesn't live in New York! She lives in …

Beth > lives in New York.
> She is 99 years old.
> She hates her city.
> She has 14 brothers.
> She wants to be an astronaut.

EXTRA Write five sentences about yourself. Make the sentences negative. Like this:

I don't live in the USA. I'm not … I …

E Das simple present: Verneinung → Grammar 1

For each sentence below, write a sentence that is negative. Like this:

I have brothers and sisters.   *I don't have brothers and sisters.*

1 Beth lives in California.
2 She likes computer games.
3 She has blond hair.
4 She's 27 years old.
5 I'm a student at a college in China.
6 I go to college seven days a week.
7 I'm extremely rich and I have four cars and a private plane.
8 There are 100 people in my class.
9 We learn German in our English lessons.
10 You come from the planet Delta III.
11 They use their phones in their lessons.
12 The students get a lunch break.

Tips and tricks
Denk daran!
Beth lives in the USA.
She doesn't **live** in Germany.
She doesn't **lives** in Germany.

F Das simple present: Fragen (to be) → Grammar 1

You are talking to Amber. Make questions for her with the verb *to be*.

1 Where / you / from?
    Where are you from?
2 What class / you / in / at high school?
3 How big / your school?
4 How old / you?
5 When / you / 18?
6 When / your birthday?
7 How far / KWCC / from your home?
8 What / your hobbies?
9 you / a sporty person?

She comes from the planet Delta III.

Check-in | Training | **More please!** | Check-out

G Das simple present: Fragen (Hauptverben) → Grammar 1
Give the missing words to make the questions.

1 Where *does* Amber *live* (live)?
2 What ... she ... (want) to do next year?
3 Why ... Americans ... (go) to a community college?
4 How long ... the courses there ... (last)?
5 How much ... they ... (cost)?
6 Where ... you ... (live)?
7 Where ... you ... (go) to college?
8 When ... your lessons ... (start) and when ... they ... (finish)?
9 What ... you ... (want) to do after college?
10 Why ... you ... (want) to have that job?

Tips and tricks
Denke daran!
He lives in the USA.
*Where does he **live**?*
*Where does he **lives**?*

H Das simple present: Fragen → Grammar 1
You are talking to an American community college student. Here are his answers to your questions – but what were your questions? Write them down.

1 My name is Romano.
  What's your name?
2 I live in Chicago, Illinois.
3 I'm 18 years old.
4 I go to college in Chicago.
5 I want to be an electrician when I finish my course.
6 I want to be an electrician because I think it's an interesting job – and my dad is an electrician.
7 There are around 5,000 students at my college.
8 I have lessons five days a week.
9 I go to college by bus.
10 It (= my course) costs $1,500.
11 Yes, I have a part-time job – I work in a fast food restaurant.
12 Yeah, I think my college is great. The teachers are all good and the course is very practical.

I Key words
Look at the words at the bottom of pages 21–25. Choose the best words to finish the sentences below.

1 – How much do the courses ...?
  – It depends. The most expensive are around $5,000.
2 A ... ... is a place where people train for jobs. In the States, these are called ... ...
3 I want to be a computer technician when I finish college. I'm on an IT ... at college.
4 I'm not at college. ... ... I'm in my room.
5 If you want to contact us, you can leave a ... on the CollegeNet website.
6 Kansas City is ... strange – it's in two states.
7 You can find out more about the college if you read this ... – it gives you all the information you need.

5 Now you

P, I **A** Look back at the message from the students at KWCC on page 20. You would like to get to know them. Post a message on the website.

1. In groups, write a message back.
2. Compare messages then write one as a class that you can post. Ask a student to write it on the board.

> Hey!
> We saw your message on the CollegeNet noticeboard.
> We are ...

Tips and tricks
The text of messages, letters and emails in English always begins with a CAPITAL letter! You can start a message like this:
Dear (name), Hi, Hey, Hello

You can finish like this:
Looking forward to hearing from you (soon).
Hoping you get back to us (soon).

P, I **B** It is two months since you first saw the message from the KWCC students and now you regularly write to them in your English lessons. Work in small groups. Choose one of the topics on the right and write a text. Put your texts up around the classroom so that students can walk round and read them (a 'gallery walk').
→ Skills 16

your town
your college
Germany
your course
your job plans
the sport(s) that you like

Video Lounge A stopover in New York

Three British students, Maya, Greg and Josh, win a film competition. Their prize is a holiday in Hollywood. In this video, the three arrive in America and have a stopover in New York before they fly to Los Angeles.

P, R, I **Watch the video and answer the questions. Compare your answers with a partner, then report to the class.**

1. How do the students travel from the airport to their hotel in New York City?
2. What three famous sights do they see on the way?
3. Who is Amy?
4. What mistake with American English does the British student Greg make?
5. What does Greg bet his friends that he can do?
6. What must his friends do at the end of the video? Why?

Check-in | Training | More please! | **Check-out**

6 Go for it!

R **A Look at the online magazine below.**

1 What is its title?
2 Who is it for?
3 How can it help you?
4 Give two examples of things you can find in the magazine.
5 What happens every day in the 'Check it out!'-section of the magazine? What is the topic today?

Go for it!

college   careers   lifestyle   tech   entertainment   advice

Go for it! magazine is the magazine for all students in Germany. It's all in English – so it will help you to practise your reading. In the magazine, you will find articles about all your favourite things and people, and tips and advice about lots of aspects of your life from college work to relationships.

The ONLINE MAGAZINE for students in Germany

CHECK IT OUT!
Every day in the magazine we highlight one topic. Today, we look at that BIG question …

How can I improve my English?

R **B Read the magazine article on page 31.**

1 Which of the writers gives these tips?
   a Use an English course from the internet.
   b Visit England.
   c Read an English book or some English magazines.
   d Try hard in lessons and do your college homework.
   e Watch films or TV in English or talk to a native speaker.

2 How did these things help the writers? Find tips that helped them to improve:
   a their listening,   d their speaking,
   b their reading,   e their writing,
   c their grammar,   f their motivation and confidence.

I, P **C Talk to a partner about the ideas below, then share your ideas in class.**

1 Look at a–f in question B2 above. Which of these things do you find most difficult in English?
2 Which of the tips in the magazine article do you find most useful?
3 Do you think you will use any of the tips in the article? Which one(s)? Why (not)?

Go for it!

college careers lifestyle tech entertainment advice

How can I improve my English?

Almost every day we get messages from our readers that say something like:
'How can I improve my English?'
Or (often!):
'Hi Leute, wisst ihr, wie ich mein Englisch schnell verbessern kann?'
We asked some of our readers who are now a bit older for their tips. Here are their answers:

Go to England. Just buy a ticket and get on a train!

Go to England. If you can, go on a language course there and stay with an English family. If you can't, just buy a ticket and get on a train! I did that before my second year at college and afterwards I liked English a lot better and had more confidence.
Patrick, Trier

Going to England is a great idea, but it costs money and when I was a student I didn't have that. Here are some things you can do at home.
- Watch television (TV series or the news) and films on DVD in English. That helps you to understand English much better when you hear it.
- If you can find an English-speaking friend or chat online on forums, it helps you to speak and write.
Yasmin, Schwerin

My English wasn't good but my older brother said: 'Read an English book or find some magazines.' I didn't understand much at first, but I got better. I learned LOTS of words and phrases and found I could understand my English lessons better. There are also books where the text is in English on one side and in German on the other.
Leonie, Berlin

There are some good English courses online. I had problems with my English grammar at college until I did an online course. It was fun and it helped me a lot.
Pascal, Bremerhaven

The best tip for learning English costs nothing. It's: Work hard in your English lessons! I know, it sounds boring. When I was at school, I had really bad marks in English. Then when I started college, I decided: I want to do better. It was a new class and a new beginning. I listened in class, tried to speak, learned new vocabulary and always did my homework. It was hard for the first six months but in the second year I was one of the best in my class in English. Now I work in my firm's office in England! I did it, so can you!
Niklas, Magdeburg

JOB PROFILE fitness trainer

What does a fitness trainer do?
A fitness trainer (or personal trainer) helps people with exercises and exercise machines. (S)he also often talks to people about their diets and a healthy lifestyle.

Where does a fitness trainer work?
A fitness trainer usually works inside in a fitness club or a sports centre.

When does a fitness trainer work?
The hours of work for a fitness trainer can be long. Fitness clubs are often open in the evenings and at weekends.

Fitness trainers usually like ...
sport, keeping fit, helping people, working with people.

A1.9

Unit 2
People and jobs

x5ww7q

Check-in | Training | More please! | Check-out

1 A careers website

P, I **A** Work in a small group. Write down in English as many jobs as you can in five minutes, then make a list in class.

P, I **B** Look at the picture on the left. The student in the picture is Daniel and he's from Australia. He wants to find out about different jobs. In your group again, answer the questions below, then report to the class.

1. What exactly is Daniel doing at the moment? For example, is he sitting in a classroom? using a laptop? listening to music?
2. Why is he doing this?
3. And YOU. What are you doing right now?

R **C** Look at the job profile on the left from a careers website. True or false? → More please! A – B

1. A fitness trainer usually works outside – for example, at a sports stadium.
2. A fitness trainer doesn't usually like sport.
3. A fitness trainer often works with people.
4. Fitness clubs are never open at the weekends.
5. A fitness trainer often talks to people about what they eat and how they live.

P, I **D** Talk in class

1. Where do you want to work one day? Do you want to work inside (for example, in an office) or outside?
2. Are you a friendly person? Do you want to work with people or to help people?

→ hours of work → usually → often → inside → outside

Tips and tricks

He **usually works** in a fitness club. The club **is often** open on Saturdays.

Adverbien wie *usually, often, always, never* usw. stehen direkt **vor** einem Hauptverb, aber **nach** *to be*.

Am Ende von Unit 2 kann ich:

— mehrere Berufe beschreiben,
— sagen, warum man gewisse Jobs vorzieht,
— sagen, was Leute oft oder gewöhnlich machen und was sie gerade im Moment machen.

Unit 2 People and jobs **33**

Check-in | **Training** | More please! | Check-out

2 Which job?

R, P   **A** Read what these four people say and the job profiles below and on page 33. What do you think? Which job is best for each person? Why?

I think the best job for person A is a … because (s)he …
Person B wants to … / likes … and so I think the best job for her / him is a …

A B C D

A
I want to work with my hands. I really like mechanical things – my hobby is go-karting.

B
I don't want to work inside. I hate offices! I like flowers and plants.

C
I love fashion and beauty. I want to work with my hands. And I'm a really friendly person. I want to meet lots of people in my job.

D
I have five small brothers and sisters. I want to work in a team and to help kids.

A 1.10

JOB PROFILE GARDENER

What does a gardener do?
A gardener looks after flowers and plants, cuts grass etc.

Where does a gardener work?
Gardeners usually work outside in gardens or parks. They sometimes also work in garden centres.

When does a gardener work?
A gardener normally works five days a week but the hours can be longer in the summer.

Gardeners usually like:
nature, being outside.

JOB PROFILE MECHANIC

What does a mechanic do?
A mechanic repairs and services cars and other vehicles.

Where does a mechanic work?
Mechanics usually work in a workshop.

When does a mechanic work?
Workshops are normally open five days a week from around 7.30 a.m. to around 6 p.m.

Mechanics usually like:
mechanical things, working with their hands, working in a team.

→ each   → normally

34

A B C D

P **B** Look at the four pictures. What are the people's jobs? What are they doing at the moment in the pictures? Use the verbs on the right.

Person A is a ... Right now he's ...

work   play
cut
sit   talk
wash
repair

P **C** Can you give the missing forms?

Das present continuous		→ More please **C – E**
I	**am**	work**ing**.
he / she / it	?	sit**ting**.
we / you / they	?	play**ing**.

JOB PROFILE NURSERY ASSISTANT

What does a nursery assistant do?
A nursery assistant looks after young children 2–5 years old. (S)he plays with children, reads stories, helps the smaller children etc.

Where does a nursery assistant work?
Nursery assistants work in private or state nurseries.

When does a nursery assistant work?
Most nurseries are open five days a week from around 7.30 a.m. to around 5.00 or 6.00 p.m.

Nursery assistants usually like:
children, working in a team, meeting and helping people.

JOB PROFILE HAIRDRESSER

What does a hairdresser do?
A hairdresser cuts men's and women's hair.

Where does a hairdresser work?
A hairdresser usually works in a salon with other hairdressers.

When does a hairdresser work?
Salons are usually open five or six days a week from around 9 a.m. to around 5 p.m.

Hairdressers usually like:
fashion and beauty, meeting people, working in a team, working with their hands.

→ to look after   → around (7.30 a.m.)   → open from ... to ...

Unit 2 People and jobs   **35**

Check-in | **Training** | More please! | Check-out

3 An interview in Australia

A A reporter from ABC Radio in Australia is in the small town of Turkey Creek today. She's interviewing Pete Collins. Pete has six jobs. What are they? Listen and put the pictures 1–6 below in the right order.

→ hunter   → to hunt   → customer

B Make sentences about Pete and his jobs. Use the phrases below.
You can listen to the interview again if you need to.

In the mornings Pete / he …

When?	What?	Where?
In the mornings	he cuts hair	in his workshop.
In the afternoons	he works as a barman	everywhere in Turkey Creek.
In the evenings	he delivers letters and packages	in his bar.
Sometimes	he repairs cars	in the river.
	he hunts crocodiles	in his shop.
	he serves customers	in his hairdressing 'salon'.

C Make questions about Pete's day. Ask another student in your class.

What does Pete do in the mornings? – In the mornings he …
Then he …
When does he cut hair? – He cuts hair …
Where does he serve customers? – He serves customers …

D Listen to these six short conversations. Which job is Pete doing at the moment? What's he doing in each conversation?

Pete is a … at the moment. He's …

E Work with a partner. Ask questions about the pictures on page 34.

What's Pete doing in this picture?
– He's delivering letters and packages.

F Talk about Turkey Creek and Pete. → More please! F – H

1 Where is Turkey Creek? In northern / southern / eastern / western Australia? Is it a big or a small town?
2 What do you think? Does Pete have a nice life? Why (not)?

Hier und dort
Einige Unterschiede zwischen Deutschland und Australien:
— **Größe:**
Deutschland 357 000 km², Australien 7,7 Millionen km².
— **Bevölkerung:**
Deutschland 82 Millionen, Australien 20 Millionen.
— **Temperatur im Dezember:**
Deutschland 5 °C, Australien 30 °C.

→ northern   → southern   → eastern   → western

Unit 2 People and jobs

4 More please!

A Das simple present mit Adverbien → Grammar 1

Decide where the adverb belongs – a) or b). Then write out the sentence in full with the adverb(s) in the correct place.

Example:
(usually) I a) ... come   b) ... to college by bike. (Answer: a)
I usually come to college by bike.
1 (often) Hairdressers a) ... work   b) ... in a salon.
2 (always) In England, shops a) ... are   b) ... open on Sundays.
3 (never) Mike is a nursery assistant. He a) ... works   b) ... on Sundays.
4 (always / often) Gardeners in big parks   a) ... are   b) ... busy but they a) ... are   b) ... particularly busy in the summer.
5 (usually / sometimes) Deb is a mechanic. She a) ... repairs b) ... cars but she a) ... repairs   b) ... motor bikes, too.

B Das simple present mit Adverbien → Grammar 1

Write these sentences again and put in the best adverbs on the right. Put the adverbs in the correct place in the sentences. More than one adverb is sometimes correct.

1 Gardeners are people who like plants and flowers.
   Gardeners are normally people who like plants and flowers.
2 Kim is a nursery assistant. She does some things every day – for example, in the afternoons, she reads her children a story.
3 Car workshops are open on Sundays.
4 When the weather is nice, the park in my town is full of people.
5 Hairdressers work in a salon but they go to people's homes, too, if the people are old or ill.
6 Fitness trainers are people who like sport and helping people. They work in a fitness club but they talk to people about diets and lifestyles, too.

sometimes
often
never
usually / normally
(almost) always

C Das present continuous (to be) → Grammar 2

Finish the sentences with the correct forms of *to be*. Use full forms *(am, is, are)*. Then choose three sentences and write them again with the short forms *('m, 's, 're)*.

1 Alison is a hairdresser. At the moment, she ... washing a man's hair.
2 The children are at the nursery. Right now, they ... playing.
3 Three gardeners ... working in the park today.
4 Jake is a secretary. He ... talking on the phone at the moment. His girlfriend Emma is at work, too. She's a fitness trainer. She ... helping a woman with an exercise machine.
5 What ... you doing at the moment? I ... learning English.

What are the kids doing at the moment?
It's 'quiet hour'. They're sleeping.

D Das present continuous (-ing forms) → Grammar 2

Copy and complete the table with the *-ing* forms of the verbs. Then use the forms to complete the sentences. Use each form only once.

to work	working	to cut	?
to do	?	to sit	?
to listen	?	to dance	?
to play	?	to use	?

1 James is a mechanic. What's he *doing* right now? He's ... in the workshop and he's ... to music on his radio.
2 The nursery assistant is ... the guitar and the children are ... .
4 Lily is ... a man's hair at the moment. The man is ... in a chair.
5 Are you ... a laptop at the moment?

E Das present continuous → Grammar 2

Finish the sentences with the *present continuous* forms of the verbs. You can use the short forms of *to be* when possible. Be careful with the spellings of the *–ing* forms!

1 Daniel *is sitting* (sit) on a beach at the moment. He ... (use) a laptop. He ... (look at) a careers website.
2 The fitness trainer ... (help) two men with an exercise. The men ... (lift) some weights.
3 James likes mechanical things. Right now, he ... (drive) a go-kart.
4 There are three hairdressers in the salon today. Two ... (cut) people's hair. One ... (wash) someone's hair.
5 The children are at the nursery at the moment. Their teacher ... (play) the guitar. The children ... (listen) and they ... (dance).
6 I ... (go) to college at the moment. I ... (sit) in a bus and I ... (do) my homework.

F Simple present oder present continuous? → Grammar 2

Finish the sentences about Pete with the right forms of the verbs. In one sentence (a or b) the verb is in the *simple present*, in the other it is in the *present continuous*.

1 (to deliver) a Pete *delivers* letters every morning.
   b It's 9 a.m. and he *'s delivering* letters at the moment.
2 (to work) a Pete ... in his bar at the moment.
   b He always ... in his bar in the evenings.
3 (to cut) a In the afternoons, Pete ... hair.
   b He ... someone's hair right now.
4 (to hunt) a Pete sometimes ... crocodiles (well, he says so!)
   b He ... a crocodile right now.
5 (to serve) a Pete ... a customer in his shop at the moment.
   b He ... customers there every day, usually in the mornings.
6 (do / repair) a What ... (Pete) at the moment? He ... a car.
   b He always ... people's cars in Turkey Creek.

So läuft's besser

Vokabellernen ist immer etwas schmerzhaft – aber das muss sein, um in der Sprache weiterzukommen. Zwei Tipps:
— Schreibe neue Vokabeln immer in ein Vokabelheft und wiederhole sie regelmäßig.
— Formuliere mit den neuen Wörtern ganze Sätze oder Redewendungen. Auf diese Weise kannst du erkennen wie sie verwendet werden und in Verbindung mit welchen Worten sie häufig auftauchen.

Unit 2 People and jobs

Check-in | Training | **More please!** | Check-out

P, R **G Simple present oder present continuous?** → Grammar 2

▲ Your class is in England and today you are visiting the kitchen of a famous restaurant. One of the chefs there is showing you round. Finish what he says. Use the *simple present* or the *present continuous*. Use your dictionary if there are words that you don't know.

Hi and welcome to our kitchen. I work here as a chef. OK, what is a typical day for us?

Well, we usually (1) *start* (start) work at 8 o'clock in the morning. We (2) ... (serve) two meals every day – lunch and dinner. Right now, at 11 o'clock, we (3) ... (prepare) lunch. On the menu today we have a special lamb with garlic sauce, so at the moment, some of my colleagues over there (4) ... (cook) the meat and some (5) ... (cut up) vegetables. And this is Marie. She (6) ... (make) the sauce. OK, we normally (7) ... (finish) serving lunch at about 2.30, and in the afternoons we are free. We (8) ... (come) back to work again at 4.30 to get ready for dinner in the evening. We finally (9) ... (finish) for the day at about midnight. Chefs (10) ... (work) very hard!

P **H Describing pictures** → Grammar 2

△ Finish the text about Pete. Use the *present continuous* to say what Pete is doing and what is happening in the scene.

In this picture, you can see Pete, the Australian man with six jobs. Pete is at the airport at the moment, he is working as a postman. He (1) *is standing* (stand) on the right. He (2) ... (hold) his bike and he (3) ... (wear) cycling shorts. In the foreground, there is a post bag with lots of letters. In the background there is a plane. It (4) ... (take off). It is a post plane.

▲ **EXTRA** Look at page 36 of your book. Describe one of the other pictures of Pete. Say where Pete is, his job right now, what you can see and where, and what the people in the picture are doing, wearing etc. Use your dictionary to look up words you don't know.

40

5 Now you

P, I **A** This questionnaire is from the CollegeNet website. Work in groups and answer the questions for you. Read your answers to the class at the end.

> Hello all college students! We'd like to have your ideas about jobs! Please write to us and give us your answers to these questions.
>
> 1 What's your name and where do you live?
> 2 Where do you go to college and what course are you on?
> 3 What things do you want in a job? (Do you want to work with your hands, to meet lots of people, … ?)
> 4 What do you want to do after college? What job do you (maybe) want to have?
>
> Just go to the CollegeNet website and post your answers on the Jobs Questionnaire page www.collegenet.com/jobsquestionnaire

JOB PROFILE POSTMAN

What does a postman do?
A postman or postwoman delivers letters, packages etc.
Where does a postman work?
…

P, I **B** Work in small groups again. Think of a job that you all know about – maybe one that you would like to have one day. Write a 'job profile'. Use the job profiles on pages 34–35 as models. Organise a 'gallery walk' or put up your profiles in the classroom. → Skills 16

Video Lounge Working as a receptionist

R, P

Sally is a receptionist in a company in England. Watch the video and finish the sentences.

1 The visitors want to see Diane Kennedy at … (time)
2 Sally asks the visitors for their …
3 Then she uses the phone to call …
4 The visitors must complete a …
5 Then Sally gives them …

Check-in | Training | More please! | Check-out

6 Go for it!

R, P **A** Look at today's magazine. What is the topic today? Do you know already what job you would like to have one day?

R **B** Read the main text on the next page. Put these ideas into the order in the text.

a talking to people about careers
b children's ideas about a career
c trying out some real jobs (working for a short time)
d questions to ask yourself when you start choosing a career
e some possible careers that aren't so 'usual'
f getting information about different jobs

R **C** Look at the part of the page called 'One man's story'.

1 a What was Mr Mancini's first job?
  b What does he do now?
  c How would people in the USA perhaps know about Mr Mancini?

2 Which of the following statements best sums up the main idea of the text?
  a Most people have the same job all their life.
  b It isn't a big problem if you can't decide now about a career.
  c You should try to find a career when you are thirty.

P **D** What do you think of the article? Does it help you to choose a career? Why (not)?

Go for it!

college **careers** lifestyle tech entertainment advice

Choosing a career

When we are young, we often say that we want to be things like a teacher, a doctor or a firefighter. But there are LOADS more careers out there. What about some more unusual careers like being a wedding planner? A DJ? A dog walker? Or a chocolate maker (a 'chocolatier')? Choosing the right career for you isn't easy!
Here are some tips.

Where do I start to choose a job?
The first step is to ask yourself some questions. What am I GOOD AT? That can include your best subjects at school or college, or it can be something like 'organising things' or 'making things with my hands'. What do I LIKE doing? That can be your hobbies or clubs. It can also be something like 'helping people' or 'being creative'. Then: WHERE AND HOW do I want to work? Inside or outside? In an office? In a shop? With other people or alone?

Perhaps chocolatier is the right job for you!

Find out about jobs
There are lots of different people who can help you with ideas about jobs. Talk to friends, family and teachers. You can get information yourself, too. Look online or at brochures and get information about different jobs. Best of all, get some 'work experience'. Working for a short time in a real job is a great way to find out if you will like it or not.

One man's story

Paul Mancini is well known around Chicago, Illinois. Paul has a 'food truck' and he sells some of the best food around – he was even in a TV programme about great food in America. But Paul spent ten years as a hospital nurse before he got his truck.

So what can Paul's story teach us? It is that people don't always know at first what they really want to be. In fact, some people only find the right job for them in their twenties or even thirties. In today's world of work, it is possible to change jobs if you don't like your first one. So, don't panic! You will find the right job in the end, but it may take time.

myface

LIBBY MILLER

PROFILE
Hometown London
Born London
Age 17
Education Student at Hatton FE College, West London
Family Mum, Dad, sister Julie

LIKES (6) see all

Carol Sharp – she writes great songs

Karate – I have my green belt!

Unit 3
Free time

9b28xu

Check-in | Training | More please! | Check-out

1 Meet Libby Miller

R, P, I **A** The girl in the photo opposite is Libby Miller. Look at the photo and at Libby's page on a social networking site called *myface*. Make notes about the questions below, compare with a partner, then report to the class.

1 What do you learn about Libby? For example, where does she live? What about her family? What are two of the things she likes?
2 Describe the photo. What do you think? Where is Libby? What is she doing there? How does she look – for example, does she look unhappy?

Hier und dort
In Unit 1 hast du einiges über *Community Colleges* in den Vereinigten Staaten gelernt. In Großbritannien heißen die Berufsschulen *Colleges of Further Education* oder verkürzt *FE colleges*.

R, P, I **B** Below are some more of Libby's 'likes' from her *myface* page.

Being a student at my college

Baking cakes

Sometimes just vegging in front of the TV

Most important – having some great friends

1 Find 'likes' that are
 · about people
 · about activities / hobbies
 · about where she studies.
2 And you? Make a list of some of your 'likes' – think of hobbies, people, places, food, sports, bands / singers, …
3 Talk about your ideas in class.

Am Ende von Unit 3 kann ich:
— über meine Freizeit reden und schreiben,
— sagen, was ich gern und nicht so gern mache,
— Dinge vergleichen,
— eine Umfrage durchführen und die Ergebnisse präsentieren.

→ FE college → social networking site → to veg

Check-in | **Training** | More please! | Check-out

2 Activities in and out of college

R **A** As in all colleges in the UK, there are lots of clubs and activities for students at Libby's college. Look at these on the college website. Find the best activities for the people below. Then say which activities interest you and why.

Molly I like being active and outdoors.
Nathan My driving test is in two months and I really need to learn the Highway Code!
Katie I love taking photos. My dream job is to be a photo journalist.
Ryan My friend almost died in an accident last year. I want to learn how to help people when things like that happen.

DRIVING TEST THEORY LESSONS These lessons will help you to prepare for the theory part of your Driving Test. Lessons are very popular so book early!
WEDNESDAYS 1 P.M. – 2:30 P.M., ROOM 214

CYCLING CLUB The cycling club organises regular cycle rides and there are mountain biking competitions. Contact: CHRIS TAYLOR AT info@hattonbike...org

THE HAT The Hat is the college online magazine and we always need writers and photographers. To find out more contact:
ANN SMITH AT: info@hatton-hat...org

RAP WORKSHOP Learn how to rap – and to write rap lyrics - in the Rap Workshop.
FRIDAYS 12 P.M. – 2:30 P.M., COLLEGE THEATRE

HENNA WORKSHOP The workshop is for all - whether you're already an expert or a complete beginner.
MONDAYS 4 P.M. – 6 P.M. ROOM 12B

FIRST AID Come and learn first aid and save lives. Courses last eight weeks.
THURSDAYS 1 P.M. – 2 P.M. MEDICAL CENTRE

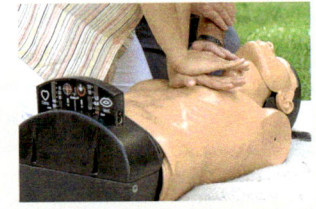

→ driving test   → Highway Code   → popular   → lyrics   → cycle ride
→ photographer   → first aid

Callum Robert George Becky

B Libby's friends are talking about the things they *like* and *don't like* doing. Copy the table below, then listen and complete it with the correct letters.

a doing karate
b swimming
c going to the gym
d making jewellery
e playing football
f playing hockey
g playing the guitar
h reading
i shopping
j watching films
k watching TV
l working on her/his car

Name	(really) likes / loves	doesn't like (so much) / isn't keen on
Callum	e, … ?	?
Robert	?	?
George	?	?
Becky	?	?

C Make sentences about Libby's friends.

Callum loves … but he doesn't like … / isn't keen on …

D Interview a partner.

1 Write two lists – things you like / things you don't like. There are some more ideas below.
2 Interview a partner and make notes.
3 Write a text about your partner and report to the class.

skateboarding · jogging · playing handball · cooking · video games · going to the cinema · swimming · being with friends · taking photos · texting friends · vegging

I really like …
I think … is brilliant.

I'm not so keen on …
I think … is boring.

What about you?
What do you like doing?

E Can you give the missing words?

Likes and dislikes → More please **A – C**

I love … to music.
I'm not … on going to the cinema.
And I … like watching TV. I think it's boring!

→ really   → brilliant   → to be keen on sth   → jewellery   → to text sb

Unit 3 Free time 47

3 A part-time job

A Here is a text which Libby posted on her *myface* page. True or false? Note down the correct answer. Correct the false sentences.

1. Libby has a part-time job in a restaurant.
2. Her job is just to make coffee.
3. Libby thinks that for her it is difficult to have a part-time job and to be a student.
4. She can usually choose the hours when she works.
5. She thinks some of her friends have better jobs than she does.
6. The most important reason why Libby likes her job is that she can earn money.

myface

My part-time job
We often talk at college about having a part-time job. Which are the best part-time jobs? When is the best time to work – in the evenings, at the weekends, in the holidays? And the most important question, is it a good idea to have a part-time job at all when you are a student?
Well, I have a part-time job. I work about eight hours a week in a coffee shop in Hatton. I'm a barista. I serve cups of coffee and tea, and sell cold drinks, cakes and snacks. I also wash up and clear tables.
So is a part-time job a good idea? For me it is, absolutely! My college work is always more important, of course, but I think I can do it and have a part-time job. The manager in the coffee shop is really nice and I can usually work my eight hours when I want to. That's great because I can fit my job around my hours at college. The job is great, too. The coffee shop where I work must be the friendliest coffee shop in Hatton. All the people who work here – and the customers – are all so friendly! Some of my friends have part-time jobs in supermarkets and shops, and I think my job here is nicer and much better than theirs. But probably the best thing of all, of course, is that I have my own money. That is just SO good!

B Look at Libby's text again. Find the missing words in these sentences, then copy and complete the table.

1. When is the … time to work?
2. And the … question, is it a good idea to have a part-time job at all?
3. Libby thinks her job is … and much better than a job in a supermarket.

Adjective	Comparative	Superlative
good	better	the ?
important	?	the ?
nice	?	the ?

→ part-time job   → to fit sth around sth   → the best thing of all
→ customer   → place

Coffee Shop

	single	double
Espresso	1.30	1.60

	regular	grande
Cappuccino	2.00	2.30
Latte	2.00	2.30
Mocha	2.05	2.35
Americano	1.70	2.00

MUFFINS (chocolate, blueberry) — 1.70

CHEESECAKE (lemon, strawberry) — 2.30

BAGELS (ham, cheese, tomato, bacon) — 2.50

LEMON CAKE — 2.10

CROISSANTS — 1.30

COOKIES (chocolate, chocolate chip, nut) — 80p

R, P C Here are some menus from Libby's coffee shop. Complete the sentences about them below. Use the *comparatives* and *superlatives* of the adjectives.

1. A single espresso is *smaller* (small) than a double espresso.
2. But a grande coffee is ... (big) than a regular coffee.
3. Of course, a grande coffee is ... (expensive) than a regular coffee.
4. The ... (expensive) kind of coffee is a mocha. The ... (cheap) coffee is a single espresso.
5. I like sweet things. Muffins are nice, lemon cake is even ... (nice), but the ... (nice) of all is cheesecake – it's my absolute favourite!

P D Make three more sentences yourself about the things on the menus – for example, say which things (snacks or coffees) you think are the nicest.

P E Can you give the missing forms?

Hier und dort

Der Vereinigte Königreich gehört nicht zur Eurozone. Die Währung, die im ganzen Königreich im Gebrauch ist, ist das britische Pfund. Ein Pfund wird in 100 Pence unterteilt. Pence wird mit p abgekürzt.

Comparatives and superlatives		→ More please **D – F**
cheap	cheaper	the cheapest
expensive	?	?
good	?	?

→ menu   → muffin   → cheesecake   → cookie (AE)   → sweet

Unit 3 Free time   49

Check-in | Training | **More please!** | Check-out

4 More please!

A Likes and dislikes

Write four sentences that are true for you.

| I | like
love
don't like
am not keen on | doing homework.
texting friends.
going on social networking sites.
doing sport.
reading newspapers.
video games.
pizza.
going to the gym.
listening to music. |

> **Tips and tricks**
> **Sagen, was man gern oder ungern macht**
> Mit *I (don't) like, I love, I'm (not) keen on* und *I hate* kann man sagen, was man gern oder ungern macht. Auf diese Ausdrücke folgt ein Substantiv oder ein zweites Verb + *-ing*.
> *I like video games.*
> *I'm not keen on watching movies.*
> *Ing*-Form Schreibregeln
> → Grammar 2

B Likes and dislikes

In this picture you can see three friends at an FE college in the north of England. Look at the table below and answer the questions about them in full sentences.

Ross   Linsey   Wes

	Ross	Linsey	Wes
☺	video games, listening to music	shopping, making clothes	swimming, reading
☹	shopping	watching the telly	video games

1 What does Ross like doing in his free time? *He likes …*
2 What isn't he so keen on?
3 What about Linsey? What are her hobbies?
4 Does she like watching TV?
5 Ross loves swimming. What else does he like doing? What doesn't he like doing?

C Likes and dislikes

1 Look at the information about the three English friends above in task B. Write two sentences about each person. Say what each one *likes, doesn't like, is keen on* or *isn't keen on*.
2 What about you? Write four sentences about what you *like* or *don't like doing*.

D Comparatives and superlatives of adjectives → Grammar 5

Note down the missing words in the table. Be careful of spellings when you see this (!).

	Adjective	Comparative	Superlative
Einsilbige Adjektive	cheap small	cheaper (2) …	(the) (1) … (the) smallest
! Adjektive mit -e am Ende	nice large	nicer (4) …	(3) … (the) largest
! Adjektive, die auf Vokal + Konsonant enden	(5) … hot	bigger (6) …	(the) biggest (the) hottest
! Adjektive mit Konsonant + -y am Ende	(7) … happy healthy (10) …	friendlier (8) … healthier easier	(the) friendliest (the) happiest (the) (9) … (the) easiest
Andere (längere) Adjektive	important expensive (13) …	(11) … more expensive more interesting	(the) most important (12) … (the) most interesting
Die Adjektive *good* und *bad*	good bad	(14) … worse	(the) best (15) …

E Comparatives and superlatives of adjectives → Grammar 5

Use adjectives from the table in D above to complete these sentences. There is sometimes more than one answer.

1. Do you like coffee or tea?
   – I like tea. I think it's much *nicer* than coffee.
2. These T-shirts cost £10. Those are much … – they're only £3.
3. This is by far the … antivirus software, and the … thing of all is that it's free.
4. I didn't like school very much. I'm much … now that I'm a college student.
5. For me, the … subject at college is maths. I love it.
6. Last year, they lost every match! They must be the … football team in the world.
7. There are … things in life than money. I think … thing is to be happy.
8. You should always eat healthy food. For example, a nice salad is much … than a burger.
9. This is the … car on the market at the moment. It's for just one person.
10. Death Valley, in eastern California, is the … place in the USA, in fact, in the world.

Welcome to Death Valley! On 10 July 1913, the temperature there was 57°C – still the world record.

P ▲ **F Comparatives and superlatives of adjectives** → Grammar 5

What do you know about London? Finish this article with the comparative and superlative forms of the adjectives.

LONDON is **(1)** *smaller* (small) than New York (8 million people live in New York and 7.7 million in London) but it is the **(2)** ... (big) city in Europe. It is also one of the **(3)** ... (important) cities in

the world for business. One of the **(4)** ... (modern) parts of London is Canary Wharf. Lots of the **(5)** ... (large) companies now have their offices here. Of course, London is also one of the **(6)** ... (famous) cities in the world for tourists. It has five airports, and millions of visitors come to London every year. The **(7)** ... (popular) places are Buckingham Palace (the home of the Queen), the Houses of Parliament, and the London Eye – the **(8)** ... (high) wheel in the world. Travelling in London is easy. There are the famous red buses and six million Londoners travel on them every day. But for tourists in London, the underground is **(9)** ... (easy) than the buses, and often **(10)** ... (quick) too. London has the **(11)** ... (old) underground system in the world: it started in 1863. It is also the **(12)** ... (large) system in Europe. Theatres, cinemas, restaurants, pubs, clubs, museums, parks, shops – London has everything. It is one of the **(13)** ... (exciting) cities in the world.

< Office workers in the morning in Canary Wharf.

^ The London underground. Londoners call it 'the tube'.

P ▲ **G Key words**

Hidden below are some of the words and phrases at the bottom of pages 45 – 49. Write out each word/phrase, then choose five words and write a sentence with each.

FECOLLEGESOCIALNETWORKINGSITETOVEGDRIVINGTEST
POPULARPHOTOGRAPHERFIR STAIDREALLYKEENTOWATCH
TVTHEBESTTHINGOFALLCUSTOMERMENUMUFFINCHEESE
CAKESWEET

5 Now you

P, I **A** A class survey. Do a survey in your class about free time activities. Make a graph, then present and talk about the results.

10 people in the class like …
2 people like …
1 person likes …
The most popular free time activity is …
Next is …
Then comes …

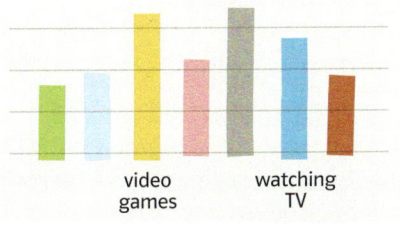

Video Lounge Go, Greg, go!

R, P Three students from Britain, Maya, Greg and Josh, win a film competition and go to the USA. In this video, they arrive in Los Angeles.
Watch the video and then finish these sentences.

1 In this video, Greg, Maya and Josh go to …
2 They go with … called Carmen.
3 Greg tells everyone that he loves …
4 He says the best country in the world in that sport is …
5 Greg makes a big mistake! He has to play … not …!
6 Things are really bad for Greg at first but he says: "Brits …"
7 At the end Greg – and everyone else – is really …

Check-in | Training | More please! | **Check-out**

6 Go for it!

R, P **A** What is the top article in the magazine today? How would you answer the question?

college careers lifestyle tech entertainment advice

What is your favourite film, book or TV series?

R **B** Read the magazine article on the next page.

1 Which reader …
   a likes science-fiction films?
   b likes a comic about a detective?
   c loves all the films of their favourite actor?
   d talks about a film in 3-D?

2 Which film, book or TV series …
   a is about some astronauts?
   b sounds 'a bit crazy' but is funny and interesting?
   c is 'always surprising'?
   d is also a video game?

R, M **C** When we talk about films, books and TV series we often put them into categories – 'types' of films, books or TV series – for example, a science-fiction film / story.

1 Find examples of some of these categories in the text.
2 Here are some types of films. Can you match the English and German?

   a adventure film   1 Dokumentarfilm
   b comedy film   2 Geschichtsfilm
   c disaster film   3 Katastrophenfilm
   d documentary film   4 Liebesfilm
   e historical film   5 Abenteuerfilm
   f romantic film   6 Komödie
   g spy film   7 Spionagefilm

P **D** Look at the 'What about YOU?'-box in the article. Tell the class your answers. Look at the readers' replies in the article for ideas and useful words and phrases.

Go for it!

college   careers   lifestyle   tech   **entertainment**   advice

What is your favourite film, book or TV series?

We all have favourites. A film we love. A TV series we watch. A book, magazine or comic we think is great. We asked our readers for their favourites. Here are some of the replies.

FILMS

My favourite film is Days of the Dead. It's an action-horror film about zombies. It's really scary and there's lots of blood!

Florian, Karlsruhe

My favourite film is a thriller called Hunt The Hunter. It's about an FBI agent who must find a man who wants to kill the American President. It's really, really exciting – and it stars my favourite actor. I love all his films!

Jessica, Erfurt

I like all science-fiction films but my favourite is Space Walk. It's about some astronauts who have to repair their spaceship in space – but there are aliens out there, too. The best thing of all is that it's in 3-D. Awesome!

Kevin, Dresden

BOOKS

My favourite book is called Vier Freundinnen. It's about four girls, best friends, who all go out with the same boy. It sounds a bit crazy, but it's about love and relationships and it's funny and interesting!

Lena, Regensburg

I like reading comics! My favourite is a crime story called Detective Dozo. There's a video game about the detective, too. Brilliant!

Philipp, Hamburg

TV series

I like lots of TV series but my favourites are Vampire City (always surprising), No Escape (scary!), and Me, My Dad and Uncle Ben (really funny!)

Franziska, Duisburg

> **What about YOU?**
>
> Do you have a favourite film, book or TV series? What is it about? Why do you like it?
> Do you have a favourite filmstar or TV actor? Who is it? Why?
> Where do you watch films – at the cinema, on DVD or blu-ray, or on internet TV (streaming media)?

Unit 4
Products and services

 Check-in | Training | More please! | Check-out

1 Bringing the world together

R, P   **A** Do you know the name of the man in the picture on the left? Read the text below for some clues!

A 1.14

In 2004, he was 23 years old and a student at Harvard University in the USA. He liked computers and, with four friends, he started a website. It was a site where students at Harvard could 'meet', get help with their university work, and talk about the things and the people they liked. He called it *The Facebook*. Soon, students at other universities joined, then American high school students – and finally people worldwide. In October 2012, *Facebook* got its one billionth user (1 billion = one thousand million). In Britain today, over half the population is on *Facebook*. In the USA it is 45 percent of the population. It is the world's biggest social networking service.

P, I   **B** Make a 'cheat sheet' for the text above. Give a short talk to the class. → Skills 15

P, I   **C** What about YOU? Write answers to these questions. Compare with a partner, then talk in class.

1 Facebook is a social networking site. Can you name other sites like it?
2 Are you on a social networking site? If 'yes', which one? When did you join? What do you do there?
   Yes, I'm on …
   I follow …
   I joined in … / last year / … ago.
   I usually / often …
3 If 'no', why not? Give two reasons.
   I'm not …
   First, I think …
   Another reason is that …

→ product / service   → to join sth

Am Ende von Unit 4 kann ich:
— über die Vergangenheit sprechen und schreiben,
— über einige bekannte Produkte und Dienstleistungen sprechen und schreiben.

Unit 4 Products and services   57

Check-in | Training | More please! | Check-out

2 Trainers then and now

A1.15

A Read this magazine article about the history of trainers.

1 When did sports shoes first start?
2 What famous company started in 1924? (Where?)
3 What important thing for trainers happened in the 1950s?

The history of trainers

top →
← sole

Plimsolls and sneakers

The first sports shoes started over 100 years ago. They were called 'plimsolls'. They had a flat rubber sole and a canvas top and they were very simple – the left foot and the right
5 foot were the same! In 1917, the U.S. Rubber Company made the first really comfortable plimsolls. They called them Keds. Soon, people called the new shoes 'sneakers'. 'To sneak' means 'to walk quietly'.

10 ### Sports shoes from Germany

In 1924, two German brothers started a sports shoe company in a small village in Germany. Their shoes had spikes and they were for athletes. The two bothers' names were Adi
15 and Rudolf Dassler. Adi called the company, yes, Adidas. Athletes used Adidas shoes in lots of Olympic Games and they were soon famous. They were the best sports shoes in the world.

20 ### Trainers and fashion

In the 1930s and 40s people wore trainers for sports like
25 athletics and basketball. Then in the 1950s a famous, young American actor, James Dean, wore trainers, jeans and a T-shirt in a movie. Trainers were now fashionable – and cheap. Soon, young people
30 everywhere wore trainers (and jeans) too.

Hi-tech trainers

In the 1960s and 70s, companies started making hi-tech trainers. The Nike company started in the USA in 1968. Nike, Adidas
35 and other companies made trainers with air in the soles of their shoes. Today, everyone loves trainers. In the USA, people buy around 350 million pairs every year!

spikes

→ history   → comfortable   → fashionable

58

B Find the missing verbs in the article.

1 The first sports shoes	started	over 100 years ago.
2 They were called 'plimsolls' and they	?	very simple.
3 Plimsolls	?	a flat rubber sole and a canvas top.
4 The U.S. Rubber Company	?	the first comfortable plimsolls in 1917.
5 The company	?	the trainers Keds.
6 But soon people everywhere	?	them 'sneakers'.
7 In 1924, Adi and Rudolf Dassler	?	Adidas.
8 Adidas trainers	?	spikes.
9 They	?	for athletes.
10 Lots of athletes	?	Adidas trainers in the Olympic Games.
11 Soon Adidas sports shoes	?	famous.
12 In the 1950s, James Dean	?	trainers and jeans in a movie.
13 After his movie, trainers	?	fashionable – and cheap!
14 Companies like Nike	?	making hi-tech trainers in the 60s and 70s.
15 These hi-tech trainers	?	air in the soles.

C Look at the verbs in exercise B. Which verbs are 'regular'? Which are 'irregular'? Make two lists.

D Make questions and answers about trainers.

1 when / first sports shoes / start
   When **did** the first sports shoes **start**? – They **started** over 100 years ago.
2 when / the U.S. Rubber Company / make the first comfortable plimsolls
3 what / people / call / Keds
4 when / Adi and Rudolf Dassler / start / Adidas
5 where / athletes / use / Adidas shoes / in the 1920s and 30s
6 why / people / wear / trainers / in the 1930s and 40s

Tips and tricks
Adidas started **in** 1924.
They wore trainers **in** the 1930s.
The first sports shoes started 100 years **ago** (= vor 100 Jahren).

E Ask the class more questions with *when*, *where* or *why*.

F Can you give the missing forms?

Das simple past			→ More please **A – D**
	regular	irregular	Fragen
	to start	to make	When ? it start?
I	started	?	What ? he wear in the movie?

→ athlete (athletics)   → company   → ago

Unit 4 Products and services

| Check-in | **Training** | More please! | Check-out |

3 The history of a company

R
A 1.16

A **Listen to Tanja Kugler and put the pictures 1–8 below in the right order.**

Tanja Kugler works for the Coca-Cola® company in Germany. She works in the Public Relations (PR) department and today she's talking to some visitors to the company. Tanja is talking about the company's history.

1

The original logo
designed by Frank Robinson

2 3

Asa Candler and
Dr John S. Pemberton

4

Coca-Cola in bottles

5

8

6 7

Coca-Cola in China Coca-Cola in cans

→ department (of a company) → pharmacist/pharmacy → assistant

Coca-Cola trucks from 1934 and the 1980s

R

B Listen again. True or false? Note down T or F.

A 1.16

1 Dr John Pemberton made the first Coca-Cola in Atlanta, Georgia, in 1886.
2 His assistant invented the name Coca-Cola.
3 Dr Pemberton sold his business to a businessman in Atlanta called Frank Robinson.
4 The famous Coca-Cola bottle started in 1960.
5 The company produced the first Coca-Cola in Germany in Frankfurt.
6 The Coca-Cola company invented Fanta in Germany in 1940.
7 The first Coca-Cola in cans was in 1982.
8 Today, people drink Coca-Cola in over 20 countries around the world.

P

C All the sentences below are wrong! Can you correct them?

1 Dr Pemberton invented the name Coca-Cola. (Frank Robinson)
*Wrong! Dr Pemberton **didn't invent** the name. His assistant Frank Robinson **invented** the name.*
2 At first, people bought Coca-Cola in bottles. (in glasses)
3 The Coca-Cola company produced the first Coca-Cola in Germany in 1999. (1929)
4 The company invented Fanta in the USA. (Germany)
5 The company sold the first Diet Coke in 2002. (1982)

P, I

D And YOU? Think of the time when you were six years old. Say three things you didn't do or didn't have then.

When I was six, I didn't speak English. I didn't have …

P

E Can you give the missing forms?

Das simple past: Verneinungen		→ More please **E – F**
I he / she / it we you they	**?**	start make invent sell drink

→ to invent   → can (of a drink)   → at first

So läuft's besser

Es gibt einige Verben, die in der Vergangenheitsform nicht auf *-ed* wie *I walked* enden: die unregelmäßigen Verben. Sie zu lernen ist einfach, wenn du dir jeden Tag ein Verb vornimmst und die Verben in Gruppen lernst wie z. B. *drink – drank – drunk* und *sing – sang – sung*. Vgl. hierzu die Auflistung im Klappumschlag.

Unit 4 Products and services

Check-in | Training | **More please!** | Check-out

4 More please!

P ▲ **A Das simple past** → Grammar 3

Finish the sentences with the *simple past* forms of the verbs. Use the irregular verb page at the back of your book to find the verbs that are irregular.

1 (make) The US Rubber Company *made* the first comfortable plimsolls in 1917.
2 (give) They ... the plimsolls the name Keds.
3 (like) People ... them very much.
4 (wear/call) When people ... the Keds they walked very quietly – so they ... them 'sneakers'.
5 (live/come) Adi and his brother Rudolf Dassler ... in Germany. They ... from a small village there.
6 (win) Athletes often ... their races because of their Adidas shoes.
7 (be) James Dean ... an American movie star in the 1950s.
8 (see/want) When young people in the 1950s ... James Dean's movies, they ... trainers (and jeans), too.
9 (start) In the 60s and 70s, companies in Europe and America ... making hi-tech trainers.
10 (buy) Now you can see trainers everywhere. Last year, Americans ... 350 million pairs.

Now everyone loves trainers.

P ▲ **B Das simple past** → Grammar 3

Test your irregular verbs! Complete the sentences with the *simple past* forms of the irregular verbs below, then check your answers with the irregular verb page at the back of your book.

1 (make) The US Rubber Company *made* the first comfortable plimsolls in 1917.
2 (be/have) They ... extremely simple – they ... just a flat rubber sole and a canvas top.
3 (feel) But they ... really comfortable and people liked them.
4 (can/give) You ... walk very quietly in them, so people ... them the name 'sneakers'.
5 (put) The Dassler brothers ... spikes on their sports shoes in the 1920s.
6 (hear/run) Many famous athletes ... about Adidas shoes and they often ... in them in their races.
7 (go) Lots of people ... to the cinema regularly in the 1950s.
8 (know) They ... the famous actors well and one of these was a young American star called James Dean.
9 (wear/think) He often ... trainers and jeans, and the young audiences ... he was really cool.
10 (buy/become) So they ... these items, too. Suddenly, trainers ... fashionable.
11 (find/sell) In the 60s and 70s, companies like Nike ... new ways to make trainers more hi-tech and they ... many millions of the new trainers.

P △ **C Das simple past (Fragen)** → Grammar 3
Below there are some facts about trainers. Complete the questions.

1 Trainers started in the USA.
   Where *did* trainers *start*?
2 The American company made the first plimsolls in 1917.
   When ... the American company ... the first plimsolls?
3 People called Keds 'sneakers' because you could walk quietly in them.
   Why ... people ... Keds 'sneakers'?
4 The Dassler brothers came from a small village in Germany.
   Where ... the Dassler brothers ... from?
5 Their shoes became famous because many athletes used them in the Olympic Games.
   Why ...?
6 Young people saw a famous actor with trainers in the 1950s.
   When ...
7 The Nike company started making hi-tech trainers in the 1960s and 70s.
   When ...?
8 Americans bought 350 million trainers last year.
   How many ...?

P ▲ **D Das simple past (Fragen)** → Grammar 3
Here are some facts about trainers. Write questions so that the facts are the answers.

1 Trainers started in the USA.
   Where did trainers start?
2 They (the U.S. Rubber Company) started making plimsolls in 1917.
3 The company called them 'Keds'.
4 But ordinary people called them 'sneakers'.
5 Adidas sports shoes had spikes on their soles.
6 Athletes often won their races because they wore the new Adidas shoes.
7 Young people in the 1950s began wearing trainers because a famous actor wore them in his movies.
8 Jeans also became popular at that time because of the same actor.
9 The Nike Company started in 1968.
10 Last year, Americans bought around 350 million pairs of trainers.

| Check-in | Training | **More please!** | Check-out |

E Das simple past (Verneinung) → Grammar 3

Jake and Jenny are both students at the same college in England but yesterday they did very different things. Read about Jake, then finish the sentences about Jenny.

1 Jake got up at 7.30. Jenny *didn't get up* at 7.30, she *got up* at 8.00.
2 Jake had coffee and toast for breakfast. Jenny ... coffee and toast, she ... muesli and orange juice.
3 Jake came to college by bus. Jenny ... to college on the bus, she ... by bike.
4 Jake had his first lesson at 9.00. Jenny ... her first lesson then, she had it at 10.30.
5 Jake ate a sandwich for lunch. Jenny ... a sandwich, she ... an apple.
6 Jake finished his lessons at 3.30 yesterday. Jenny ... finish at 3.30, she ... at 5.30.
7 In the evening, Jake went on Facebook. Jenny ... on Facebook, she ... (watch) a DVD.
8 Jake sent texts to his friends, too. Jenny ... texts to her friends – she ... (phone) them.

F Das simple past (Verneinung) → Grammar 3

Do exercise E above, then write about three more things that Jake and Jenny did differently yesterday. Write sentences like those in exercise E. Here are some ideas to get you started.

do a test in an English lesson · go to the gym after college · ...

G Key words

Look at the words at the bottom of pages 57–61. Use them to translate the sentences below into English.

1 Facebook und Twitter sind Soziale Netzwerke im Internet.
2 Wann bist Du Facebook beigetreten?
3 Die Firma hat eine interessante Geschichte.
4 Chrissy kleidet sich sehr modisch.
5 Mein Bruder arbeitet in der Marketingabteilung einer großen Berliner Firma.
6 Ein Apotheker arbeitet in einer Apotheke.
7 Ich hätte gerne eine Dose Cola.
8 Steven Sasson erfand die Digitalkamera *(digital camera)* 1975.

5 Now you

R, P, I **A** The text below is about the invention of mobile phones – but some information is missing. Work with a partner.

Partner A: Please look at page 105 now.
Partner B: Answer your partner's questions. Then ask your questions to find the missing facts in this article.

This man's name is Dr Martin Cooper. He invented the modern mobile phone. He tested it for the first time on 3 April (1) ... (year). On that day, he made the first phone call in (2) ... (city). Ten years later, the Motorola company produced the first commercial mobile phones – mobile phones that everyone could buy. They (3) ... (had? didn't have?) text messaging or cameras. They weighed over 1 kilogram! And in today's money they cost around (4) $ ... !

M **B** Your friend wants to know about the products and services in this unit but doesn't speak English. Choose one text and give your friend the most important information in German.

Video Lounge Making movies

R **Watch the video.
True (T) or false (F)?**

1 In the first scene, the three students are making a movie.
2 It is a science-fiction movie.
3 Josh shoots Greg in the leg.
4 The blood in the packet is not real blood.
5 In film studios, they can make a hole in clothes with a remote control.
6 Greg must carry a transmitter in his pocket.
7 The director can't stay because he is making a movie next door.
8 Unfortunately, the three students can't watch him at work in the studio.
9 Before they leave, Maya has to give back the shoes she wore in the movie.

Unit 4 Products and services

| Check-in | Training | More please! | **Check-out**

6 Go for it!

R, P **A** Look at the magazine. What is the top article today? Write down three ideas about the topic on a piece of paper, then tell the class. Use the phrases below.

college   careers   lifestyle   tech   entertainment   advice

Feeling good, looking good

If you want to be fit and healthy, it is important to …
You should … You shouldn't … It is a bad idea to …

R **B** Read the magazine article. Say if the statements below are true or false according to the text.

1 Being fit and healthy is good for your body but it is also good for the way you think and feel.
2 You should try to get some exercise two or three times a week.
3 The most important thing about exercise is that it feels 'hard'.
4 Watching TV and playing video games are not good because you sit down for too long.
5 Foods like apples and carrots are an important part of your diet.
6 You should never eat burgers or other fast food.
7 Doctors now think that too much fat in foods is a big reason why so many people are overweight.
8 If possible, you should stop drinking soft drinks because they contain a lot of sugar.
9 Some people think that smoking is cool – but they are wrong.

P **C** So how fit and healthy are you? Answer the questions below with 'yes' or 'no'. Then write two things that you think you should do (or want to do) in the future to be fitter and healthier.

1 I get some exercise every day.
2 I regularly do a sport or swim.
3 I go to a gym at least three times a week.
4 I watch a lot of TV.
5 I often play computer and video games for a long time.
6 I always eat lots of fresh fruit and vegetables.
7 I eat fast food at least three times a week.
8 I never drink soft drinks.
9 I smoke.

In the future, I think I should / shouldn't …

Go for it!

college careers **lifestyle** tech entertainment advice

Feeling good, looking good

Feeling good is important for everyone, but for teens it is very important. If you feel fit and healthy, you feel more positive, can work better, and life doesn't feel so stressful. And, of course, if you are fit and healthy, you look great! So what are the most important things to do? Here are our ideas.

Get plenty of exercise
Exercise should be a part of your daily life like eating, sleeping and going to college. Try to get some exercise every day for 20 to 30 minutes. You can get exercise when you play a sport, swim, cycle, go to the gym, or just work out in your room at home. The most important thing is that it's fun! Some people like playing in a team, or being in a club. That way, they can exercise with their friends.

A healthy lifestyle
Being fit and healthy is not just about going to a gym. You need a healthy lifestyle in general.
- We all like watching TV, using our computer and playing video games. But if you spend too long just sitting down, it is not good for your health (and remember, you sit down at college and when you do homework, so it is very important that you find time to exercise).
- Eat regularly, three times a day, and make sure you eat plenty of fresh fruit and vegetables.
- We read a lot about 'junk food' and that it is very unhealthy. The problem is that we all love burgers, fries and other kinds of fast food! It is OK to have some fast food sometimes – when you are out with your friends, for example. But just remember that it is full of bad things like fat, salt and sugar, so don't eat it every day.

Doctors now think that one of the most important reasons why so many people are overweight is that they get too much sugar, and one thing that is full of sugar is soft drinks. If you can, stop drinking them at all. If you can't, drink the low-sugar sorts of drinks.
And finally, don't smoke, drink alcohol or take drugs. Doing those things is NOT cool! It is very, very dangerous!

Make sure you eat plenty of fresh fruit and vegetables!

Unit 4 Products and services

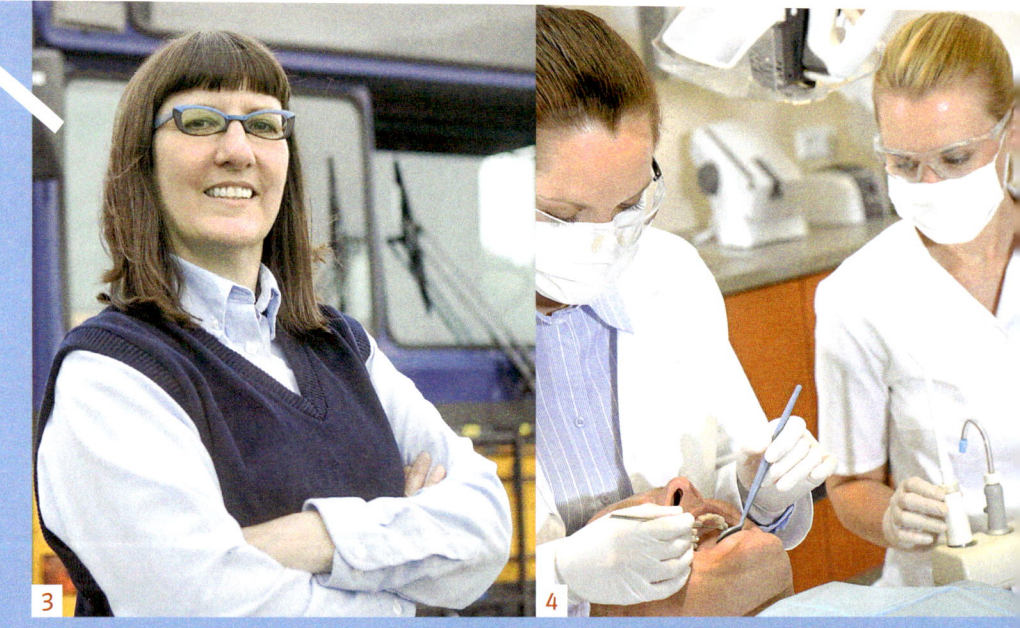

Unit 5
Dos and don'ts at work

Check-in | Training | More please! | Check-out

1 Different jobs, different rules

R **A** **Look at the pictures on the left and find:**

a shop assistant / a construction worker / a dental assistant /
a bus driver

R **B** **In every job there are 'rules' – things you must (or mustn't) do. Match these rules to the jobs in the four pictures.**

1 Someone in this job must (or: has to) drive carefully. They mustn't drive too fast, for example.
2 In this job, you must (or: have to) be polite to your customers. You mustn't be rude to them! "The customer is always right!"
3 A person in this job must / has to have very clean hands because hygiene is important. (S)he mustn't have dirty fingers.
4 People in this job must / have to wear a hard hat at work. They mustn't work without one.

R, P **C** **In different jobs there are also different things that aren't so important. The construction worker on the left is Sam. The dental assistant is Katie. Who is this – Sam or Katie?**

1 This person doesn't have to wear a hard hat at work.
   That's …
2 This person doesn't have to have very clean hands.

> **Tips and tricks**
> Vorsicht!
> *you mustn't* = du **darfst** nicht
> *you don't have to* = du **musst** / **brauchst** nicht

M **D** **Translate the six sentences in exercises B and C above into German. Compare with a partner, then tell the class.**

R, I **E** **Think about the rules at your college. Finish these sentences in your own words, then talk in class.**

1 At my college, we must / have to …
2 We mustn't …
3 But we don't have to …

→ rule → assistant → hard hat → important

> **Am Ende von Unit 5 kann ich:**
> — über Regeln am Arbeitsplatz reden und schreiben,
> — Schilder am Arbeitsplatz verstehen,
> — über mögliche Konflikte am Arbeitsplatz reden und schreiben.

Unit 5 Dos and don'ts at work **69**

Check-in | Training | More please! | Check-out

2 Signs at work

R **A** There are lots of signs at work – in offices, in factories, in shops, in car parks, and on construction sites. Look at the signs on the next page. Find a sign or signs ...

1 about something you wear on your ears.
2 about something you wear on your eyes.
3 about smoking.
4 about the floor in a shop.
5 about electricity.
6 for car and lorry drivers.
7 about a construction site.
8 about your bags at an airport.
9 about fire.
10 about a small vehicle that transports heavy things.
11 about mobile (cell) phones.
12 for visitors to an office or a factory.

That's sign C (D, L, ...).

R, P **B** Make two lists. Which signs say things you *must / have to do* and which signs say things you *mustn't do*?

must / have to	mustn't
sign N, ...	sign A, ...

P **C** Make sentences about the signs. Use the verbs and phrases below.

use · smoke · wear · leave · be careful because there is / are ... · break · go · park your car · stop · drive faster than

Sign A means you mustn't smoke.

P **D** Look at the sign on the right. It's on the noticeboard in an office in the USA. Can you explain – what is 'Casual Friday'? (Tip: you wear 'casual clothes' like jeans and T-shirts at home. In offices, people normally wear 'formal clothes' like suits and skirts.) Think about *must / have to, mustn't* and *don't have to*.

REMEMBER!

TOMORROW IS CASUAL FRIDAY

→ electricity → lorry → to transport → to break → noticeboard

P **E** Can you give the missing forms?

Must und have to				→ More please **A – F**
I			have to	don't have to
he she it	must	mustn't	?	?
we you they			have to	don't have to

→ caution → danger → in case of (fire) → Keep out!

Unit 5 Dos and don'ts at work

Check-in | Training | More please! | Check-out

3 Conflicts at work

A 1.17

JOB MAG is a magazine in Britain for young people in their first years at work. There are articles about careers, interviews, news stories … and much more. There is also a letter page where people can write if they have problems in their workplace. Here are two letters to the Job Mag problem page. Read the letters below and do task A on page 73.

Dear JOB MAG
I am 19 years old and I work as a receptionist in a dental practice in my town. Together with three other women, I work at the reception
5 desk, answer the phone, put appointments into the computer and so on. Because we are a small team, we also have to share lots of other smaller jobs – we make tea and coffee for the dentists, for example, take letters to the post
10 office at the end of the day, sometimes go to the bank for cash – and so on. The problem is that one woman in our team, Judith, is a bit older and thinks she is 'better' than us younger girls. She refuses to do these smaller jobs. I love my work generally but Judith is a real problem for me.
15 Can you help?   **Cheryl, Manchester**

Dear JOB MAG
I am a shop assistant in a sports shop in my town. It is part of a big national chain. I started work there last year and at first I loved the job. But then six months
5 ago, I began to get angry about my work and now I am very unhappy. The problem is our manager. There are five assistants in the store and the manager likes two of them and doesn't like the others. I'm one of the assistants he doesn't like! With his two favourites (one
10 of them is the son of the manager's friend) he's always nice and they get all the interesting jobs. On the other hand, the three of us all get the not-so-nice jobs: we have to clean the floor, for example, and move around all big boxes of sports goods. I don't really want to have
15 to look for a new job but at the moment I hate going to work in the shop. Please help!   **Robert, Bristol**

→ workplace   → appointment   → to refuse (to do sth)   → chain (of shops)

R, P, I **A** True or false? Note down T or F, then compare answers in class. When a sentence is wrong, give a correct sentence.

1 Cheryl is a receptionist and Robert is a shop assistant.
2 Cheryl has a problem with her two young colleagues.
3 Robert's problem is with his shop manager.
4 Judith works well in the team and shares all the work with the others.
5 In Robert's shop, the manager's favourites don't have to do the more difficult jobs.
6 Cheryl doesn't like her work but she likes Judith.
7 Robert plans to look for a new job.

R, P, I **B** Here are the magazine's answers to the two letters. Work with a partner or in a small group. Make 'to-do' lists for Cheryl and Robert according to the magazine. Compare your answers in class.
A 1.18

Dear Cheryl
It is particularly important in a small office that everyone works together. First, you must talk to your two younger colleagues. If they feel like
5 you (and I think they will!), go and talk to Judith together. Explain how you feel and ask Judith about her feelings. Remember: you mustn't get angry! Problems often happen at work and you can usually solve them if you talk. If Judith still
10 refuses to share jobs, then you must go to the practice manager or one of the dentists.

Dear Robert
I understand why you are unhappy. Usually, it is best to talk to the person who is your 'problem', but in your situation, I think you have to talk to someone
5 who is 'higher' than your boss. Your shop is part of a big, national chain. Write to the head office. They will probably talk to your boss and perhaps to your other colleagues if they are also unhappy. Before you contact the company, you must also write down
10 examples of the things you are unhappy about – what happened, dates etc. The situation in your shop is unfair and you don't have to put up with it.

talk to my ...

explain how ...

P, I **EXTRA** Choose one of the letters. For Cheryl, act out the discussion with Judith. For Robert, write a letter to his head office.

→ head office   → probably   → to put up with (sth)

Check-in | Training | **More please!** | Check-out

4 More please!

A must (have to) / mustn't → Grammar 8

Write down a) or b).

1 In England you a) must   b) mustn't drive on the left.
2 But you a) have to   b) mustn't drive on the left in Germany!
3 On construction sites, workers usually a) have to   b) mustn't wear hard hats.
4 You a) must   b) mustn't smoke where you see a 'no smoking' sign.
5 In many offices nowadays, workers a) have to   b) mustn't go outside to smoke.
6 Lorry drivers drive long distances. Sometimes they a) have to   b) mustn't be away from home for a week or more.
7 Sorry. Customers a) must   b) mustn't bring dogs into the shop.
8 Chefs a) have to   b) mustn't work in hot kitchens. And often they a) must   b) mustn't work in the evenings and at weekends too.

B must / has to / doesn't have to → Grammar 8

Finish the text about Ed.

Ed is an office worker in New York. From Monday to Friday he **(1)** ... travel to work on the subway. He **(2)** ... wear a suit and a tie and he **(3)** ... work from 9 a.m. to 5 p.m. in his office. But Saturday and Sunday are different. Ed **(4)** ... travel on the subway and he **(5)** ... wear a suit or a tie. In the summer, he usually goes to the beach on Coney Island. He swims in the sea and relaxes. He **(6)** ... work. It's great!

Office workers 'enjoy' smoking nowadays!

C mustn't / don't have to → Grammar 8

Give the missing words.

1 The sign says: 'No parking'. That means you ... park here.
2 This software is free. You ... pay for it.
3 He won 70 million euros on the lottery so he ... work.
4 The meeting starts at 11.00. Be there punctually! You ... be late!
5 Listen carefully. You ... forget this, it's important.
6 You can do that if you want – but you ... You can decide.
7 Mobile phones are forbidden here. Pupils ... use them in class!
8 Companies sometimes say: 'Pay in 30 days.' In other words, customers ... pay immediately.

D must (have to) / mustn't / don't have to → Grammar 8

Serkan is from Bochum in Germany. Last month, he finished his business course at college. Now he is in Birmingham, Britain's second largest city. He has a work placement *(Praktikum)* in a British media company. It makes films for TV and sells them around the world. Serkan is in the export department. It is Serkan's first day in the office. Read his job description and the office rules, then say if the sentences below are true or false. When a sentence is false, write a correct sentence. Use *has to*, *doesn't have to* or *mustn't*.

JOB DESCRIPTION
- Work from 9.00 a.m. to 5.30 p.m. Monday to Friday. Weekends are free.
- Answer the telephone.
- Translate letters and emails from our German customers.
- Write letters and emails in German to our German customers.

OFFICE RULES
Please do …
- Ties and suits are not necessary but please be dressed smartly at all times.
- Be punctual.
- Turn off your computer at the end of the day.

Please don't …
- Don't use the office telephone for private calls.
- Don't send or receive personal emails.
- Don't eat at your desk.
- This is a no-smoking office.

1 Serkan has to start work each day at 9 o'clock. *True*
2 He has to work on Saturdays.
  False. He doesn't have to work on Saturdays.
3 When the telephone on his desk rings, he has to answer it.
4 Serkan can use the phone on his desk to phone his parents in Germany.
5 He doesn't have to turn off his computer at 5.30.
6 He has to wear a suit and tie at work.
7 He has to write letters to the company's British customers.
8 He mustn't eat sandwiches at his desk.
9 He can smoke in the office.
10 He has to arrive punctually at work each day.
11 He can email his old college friends in Germany from his computer.
12 He has to translate German letters and emails into English.

E must (have to) / mustn't / don't have to → Grammar 8

EXTRA Serkan wants to tell his friends in Germany about his job and the rules in his office. Write an email for him in German (which he can send from his own computer of course!).

Check-in | Training | More please! | Check-out

P **F must (have to) / mustn't** → Grammar 8

▲ Serkan has his car with him in Birmingham so he has to know about English road signs and traffic lights. Write a sentence about each of these signs. Use the phrases below the signs. Tip: the speed limit *(Geschwindigkeitsbegrenzung)* in British towns is 30 miles per hour (mph).

- This sign means that you …
- When you see this sign you …
- You … when you see this sign / when the traffic lights are …
- you can / you are allowed to …
- you have to / you must …
- you mustn't / you aren't allowed to / it is forbidden to …

P **G Key words**

▲ Look at the words at the bottom of pages 69–73. Choose the best words to finish the sentences below.

1. ... tell you the things you must or mustn't do. One ... at my college is 'No smoking in the college'.
2. A ... is a large vehicle that transports goods. In German it's called an 'LKW'.
3. When you see the word '...' on a sign, it means you must be careful.
4. In hotels, you often see the sign: 'Don't use the lift ... ... fire'. That means you mustn't use it when there is a fire.
5. If you see a sign on a door that says: '... ...!' it means you mustn't go into that room.
6. (Man to receptionist in an office) 'Good morning. I have an ... with Ms Westbury at 10.30.'
7. McDonalds is an international ... of fast food restaurants.
8. 'No! I ... to do that!'
9. We have offices around the UK but our ... ... is in London.
10. You don't have to ... ... things in your workplace that are unfair! Talk or write to someone about the situation.

5 Now you

I, P **Being a college student is very different from working in a job. Work with a partner or in a small group and do the tasks below. Then compare your answers in class and talk about college and working.**

1 Write down two things you have to do at college but that you don't have to do when you have a job.
2 Write down two things you maybe have to do when you have a job but that you don't have to do when you are a student.
3 Write down one reason why being at college is perhaps better than having a job.
4 Write down one reason why having a job is perhaps better than being at college.
5 What do you think? Which is better? College or a job? Why?

Video Lounge Working as a PA

A PA is a Personal Assistant. Jasmine Goodman is a PA in the same firm as Sally (Unit 2). She works for Ms Kennedy. She is looking after the two visitors. They are in Ms Kennedy's office.

R, P **Watch the video and answer the questions.**

1 Ms Kennedy is not there. Why not?
2 Jasmine offers the visitors something to drink while they are waiting. What drinks do they choose?
3 One of the visitors tells Jasmine that she doesn't have to call him Mr Rogers. What can Jasmine call him?
4 Jasmine says to the visitors that she is sorry they have to … (what?). How do they reply?

Unit 5 Dos and don'ts at work   77

6 Go for it!

A Look at the magazine. What is the top article today? Complete the sentence below with an idea of your own, then tell the class.

Go for it!

college   careers   lifestyle   tech   entertainment   advice

What is a good friend?

A good friend is someone who …

B Read the magazine article on the next page and choose the correct answer a, b or c below.

1 It isn't … to be a good friend.
   a a good idea
   b hard
   c easy

2 Being dependable means that …
   a you help your friend when he or she helps you.
   b you always help your friend.
   c you help your friend when it is easy for you.

3 You must always tell a friend …
   a what you think.
   b what other people think.
   c what your friend wants to hear.

4 Good friends …
   a always agree.
   b sometimes disagree.
   c always have the same ideas.

5 You should say sorry …
   a if you make a mistake.
   b if your friend makes a mistake.
   c if you are unhappy.

6 'Using' a friend means that …
   a you help her or him all the time.
   b your friend doesn't help you.
   c your friend helps you but you don't help her or him.

7 You should …
   a always be on your friend's side.
   b never criticise other people.
   c always listen to gossip.

C Write a short story called *A good friend*.

Think of a time when someone was a good friend for you. It can be a real situation, or you can invent a story. Think about these keywords:
· Who (are the people in the story)?
· When (did the story happen)?
· Where (did the story happen)?
· What (happened)?
· Why (was this person a good friend on that day)?

Go for it!

college   careers   lifestyle   tech   entertainment   **advice**

What is a good friend?

Having a good friend makes you a happier person. But if you want to have a good friend, you must also be a good friend. Being a good friend isn't easy. It takes time and some hard work. So, how do you be a good friend? Here are some ideas to think about.

Be dependable
Being 'dependable' means that your friend knows that you are always there for her or him. Not just when it is easy for you, but when things are difficult. If your friend has a problem, then you are there to help. Always.

Be honest
A good friend is someone who tells you the truth. Of course, you have to be careful when you say things. Being honest doesn't mean saying: 'You're an idiot!'. But you must always know that you can talk to a friend about things that are difficult, and that your friend will tell you what he or she thinks.

Have respect for your friend
Your friend has some new clothes which you don't like. Or your friend believes something and you don't agree. You can be honest about your opinion, but in the end, you must accept that your friend has a different idea. You can agree to disagree!

Say sorry
We all make mistakes. No one is perfect! A good friend must understand this. If you make a mistake, say sorry and show that you feel bad because you made your friend unhappy.

Don't gossip about a good friend behind their back.

Don't 'use' your friend
Friends do things for each other, but that doesn't mean that you can 'use' your friend. If your friend helps you, you must also help him or her.

Be loyal
This is one of the most important things in a good friendship. It can be very easy to criticise a friend when she or he isn't there – to talk about your friend 'behind their back'. People love to gossip, but you mustn't do this about your friend. Being 'loyal' means that you are always on your friend's side, even if that is sometimes difficult.

LOCAL SUCCESS STORY

Do you need a plumber? What about new windows? A patio in your garden maybe? Then ring Lucas Nowak.

A 1.19

Lucas is from Poland – his real name is Lukasz. But he has lived in Danbury since 2008. And he has had his own building firm here for three years.

"When I first came to England," says Lucas "I wanted to stay maybe a year or two just to earn some money. But now I want to stay in Danbury. The people are very friendly and my new life here is very good."

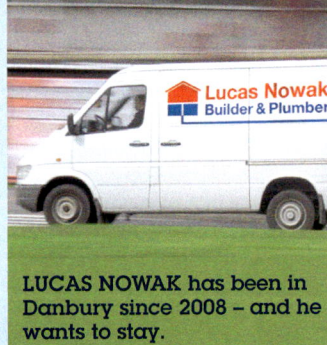

LUCAS NOWAK has been in Danbury since 2008 – and he wants to stay.

Unit 6
Success stories

Check-in | Training | More please! | Check-out

1 A new life

R, P **A Read about Lukasz and answer the questions.**

Lukasz Nowak was born in Poland. But in 2008, when he was 24, he moved to England. He now lives in a town in England called Danbury. Lukasz worked in Danbury first as a plumber. Then three years ago, he started his own small building firm. He now has six employees. His firm is very successful. Everybody in Danbury knows 'Lucas'.

1 Where was Lukasz born?
2 When did he move to England? What town does he live in?
3 What was Lukasz's first job in Danbury?
4 What did he do three years ago?

Hier und dort
Großbritannien ist ein multikulturelles Land – in London werden über 300 verschiedene Sprachen gesprochen. In den 1960er Jahren wanderten viele Menschen aus Indien, Pakistan, China oder der Karibik ein. Seit 2004 gibt es auch viele Einwanderer aus Mitteleuropa – wie Lukasz.

R **B The article on the left is from the local newspaper in Danbury. Look at it now and find the missing verbs for the diagram below.**

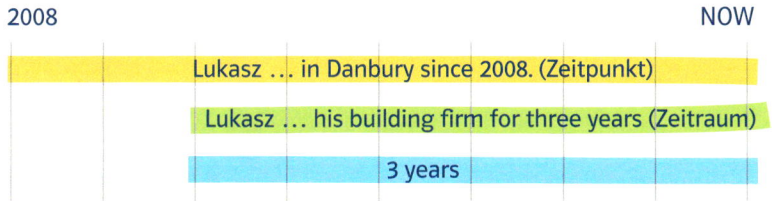

Lukasz has ... since ...
He has ... for ...

Tips and tricks
since 2008 = Zeitpunkt
for three years = Zeitraum
Vorsicht! Auf Deutsch heißen *since* und *for* beide ‚seit'!

M **C Your friend wants to know about the article but (s)he doesn't speak English. Give the most important ideas in German.**

→ to move → (his) own (firm) → employee → local
→ to earn (money)

Am Ende von Unit 6 kann ich:
— mitteilen, seit wann etwas schon andauert,
— über Erfolgsgeschichten reden und schreiben.

Unit 6 Success stories **81**

Check-in | Training | More please! | Check-out

2 A magazine article

A Read this magazine article about a famous British chef. Find out …

1 Why was Jamie no good at school?
2 Who are the young people with Jamie in the photo at the top?
3 Who is the woman with him in the second photo?

Jamie and Jools

No good at school but great at his job

Jamie Oliver makes cooking cool. He's famous now and he's often on TV – and not just in Britain but around the world. But Jamie wasn't a good pupil at school! Here's his success story.

Jamie was born in the south-east of England in 1975. His mum and dad had a pub and Jamie started helping in the kitchen there when he was eight. School was hard for Jamie – he's dyslexic – but after school, when he was 16, he went to a college in London and trained to be a chef. Jamie was a brilliant college student. He left college in 1992. He worked in some famous restaurants in France, and then in London. In 1998, a British TV company made a film about one of the London restaurants. Everybody saw Jamie on TV and soon he was the star of the show. Jamie Oliver, the unsuccessful pupil, was famous!

Jamie opened his first restaurant in London in 2002 – but it wasn't a normal restaurant. He found 15 unemployed young people and trained them. The young people had lots of problems and it was hard work, but they were successful. They are now chefs in the restaurant. The restaurant is called *Fifteen* because there were 15 young chefs. Then Jamie trained more young people in England, Holland and Australia.

Jamie is married. He met his wife Juliette (Jamie calls her 'Jools') at school. He married her in 2000. They live in London and have four children.

→ to train to be a … → chef → to leave (college) → unemployed → dyslexic

82

R **B** Which is right? Note down a, b or c.

1. Jamie Oliver was born
   a in the north of England.
   b in the south-west of England.
   c in the south-east of England.
2. He first worked in a kitchen
   a at school.
   b in his parents' pub.
   c at college.
3. Jamie trained to be a chef
   a in London.
   b in France.
   c in the USA.
4. He was first on TV
   a in 1975.
   b in 1987.
   c in 1998.
5. Jamie trained 15 … people for his *Fifteen* restaurant in London.
   a successful young
   b unemployed old
   c unemployed young
6. Jamie now has *Fifteen* restaurants in … countries.
   a two
   b three
   c four
7. Jamie first met his wife … and they have …
   a in 2000 / three children.
   b at college / two children.
   c at school / four children.

P **C** Finish the *How long …?* sentences about Jamie.

	Then	Now	How long …?
1	Jamie first worked as a chef in 1992.	He works as a chef now.	He *has* worked as a chef *since* 1992.
2	Jamie was first famous in 1998.	He's famous now.	He … been famous … 1998.
3	Jamie had his first *Fifteen* restaurant in London in 2002.	He has a *Fifteen* restaurant in London now.	He … a *Fifteen* restaurant in London … 2002.
4	He had his first *Fifteen* restaurant in Australia in 2006.	He has a *Fifteen* restaurant in Australia now.	He has had a *Fifteen* restaurant in Australia for … years.
5	Jamie married Jools in 2000.	He's married to Jools now.	He has been married to Jools … years.

I **D** Ask and answer questions with a partner like those on the right.

P **E** Can you give the missing forms?

Das present perfect		→ More please **A – E**
I	have	worked
he / she / it	?	been
we you they	?	lived had

How long has Jamie Oliver worked as a chef?

He has worked as a chef since …

How long has he …?

He has …

→ successful   → to marry   → to be married to (someone)

Unit 6 Success stories

Check-in | **Training** | More please! | Check-out

3 We have our own firm!

R **A Read about Kate, Annie and Ruth.**

1 Where do they live?
2 Where were they all students?
3 What did they do after college?
4 What does their firm do?

Ruth

Kate and Annie

Kate, Annie and Ruth live in Danbury in England – the same town as Lukasz Nowak. They were all students – and best friends – at Danbury FE college. When they left college, they started their own firm in the town. It's called PartyPeople. The firm organises parties (with food and music) for schools, local firms and local kids.

R, P   A1.21 **B A reporter from the Danbury newspaper is interviewing Kate, Annie and Ruth about their firm. He has these questions for them. Listen and find the answers.**

Questions for Kate, Annie and Ruth
1 How old are you?
2 What courses were you on at college?
3 How long have you had the firm 'PartyPeople'?
4 What are your different jobs in the firm?
5 How (where etc.) did you start the firm?
6 How long have you been in your office?

→ cookery   → electronics   → customer

R, P **C** You're the reporter now. Finish your article about Kate, Annie and Ruth.

Three Danbury women and their successful company

Do you want a party? Do you need food? Music? The local firm PartyPeople can organise everything for you!

Kate, Annie and Ruth are now **(1)** ... years old. They were all friends and students at **(2)** ... College. Kate was on a **(3)** ... course, Annie on a **(4)** ... course and Ruth wanted to be a **(5)** ... When they left college, they started their firm, PartyPeople. They have had the firm now for **(6)** ... years.

The three women all have different jobs in the company. **(7)** ... is the 'businesswoman',

(8) ... is the disk jockey who plays the music, and **(9)** ... cooks all the food for the parties.

PartyPeople is very successful now. But it was small when it started. At first, Kate, Annie and Ruth organised the parties and cooked the food in Kate's **(10)** ... Now the three women use an old pizzeria in Danbury. They cook the food in the kitchen and the **(11)** ... is their office. They have been in the pizzeria for **(12)** ... years.

I, P **D** Interview your partner. → More please! F

1 First copy and fill in the form for YOU.
2 Then interview a partner. Write in your partner's answers.
3 Write a short text about your partner.

My partner … (name) lives in … (S)he's lived there for / since …

		YOU	Your partner
1	What street do you live in? How long have you lived there?	?	?
2	What's your favourite band? How long have you liked it?	?	?
3	What's your favourite piece of clothing? How long have you had it?	?	?
4	Do you have a car, a bike or a scooter? How long have you had it?	?	?
5	How long have you learned English?	?	?

So läuft's besser
Für das *present perfect* brauchst du noch die unregelmäßigen Verben im Klappumschlag. Dieses Mal geht es um die 3. Form:
to be – was / were – **been**
to go – went – **gone**

→ to organise   → to fill in a form   → piece of clothing

Unit 6 Success stories   **85**

4 More please!

A since / for → Grammar 4

Since or *for*? Finish the sentences.

1 Lukasz Nowak has lived in England ... 2008.
2 He has had his own firm ... the last 3 years.
3 Jamie Oliver has been a famous chef ... over 20 years.
4 He has been married to Jools ... 2000.
5 Greg is an English college student. He has been at college ... last September.
6 He's at college now. He has been there ... 9.00 this morning.
7 It's midday now so he has been there ... 3 hours.

B Present perfect with since / for → Grammar 4

Answer the questions with complete sentences. Be careful with *since* and *for*!

1 How long has Lukasz Nowak lived in England? (2008)
  He (Lukasz) has lived in England since 2008.
2 How long has Jamie Oliver been a chef? (over 20 years)
3 How long have you been married, Jamie? (2000)
  I ...
4 How long have Jamie and Jools lived in London? (12 years)
5 How long have you worked in a *Fifteen* restaurant, Laura? (2011)
6 How long has David been a chef? (3 years)

C Present perfect / simple present / simple past → Grammar 1, 3, 4

In sentences a), b) and c), one verb is in the *simple present*, one in the *simple past*, and one in the *present perfect*. Give the right forms.

1 a Lukasz *lives* (live) in Danbury.
  b He *moved* (move) to Danbury in 2008.
  c He ... (live) in Danbury since 2008.

2 a Jamie Oliver ... (leave) college in 1992.
  b He ... (be) a chef now.
  c He ... (be) a chef since 1992.

3 a Laura ... (be) a chef in a *Fifteen* restaurant.
  b She ... (start) working there 18 months ago.
  c She ... (worked) there now for 18 months.

He's been a chef for three years but before that he worked in a circus.

Name:	Nadine Zimmermann
Age:	19
Born:	Krefeld, Germany
Family:	Father Rolf, Mother Angelika
3 years ago:	Family left Krefeld and moved to St. Louis, Missouri, USA. Father got job as police officer
Last year:	Nadine finished high school in St. Louis and became a student on a business course at a community college there
Six months ago:	Mother got a job as a nurse in hospital in St. Louis. Nadine met Ben, (her "true love"!), another student on her course

R, P ▲

D Present perfect / simple present / simple past → Grammar 1, 3, 4

I live in America now! Read the 'quick facts' about Nadine and answer the questions below. Be careful to use the right tenses!

1 Where was Nadine born?   *She …*
2 Where does she live now?
3 When did she leave Germany?
4 What city in the USA did she move to?
5 What is her father's job there?
6 How long has he had that job?
7 What is her mother's job?
8 How long has she had that job?
9 What kind of school did Nadine go to first in St. Louis?
10 Where is Nadine a student now and what course is she on?
11 How long has she been a student there?
12 How long has Nadine known Ben? Why is he important in her life?

R, P ▲

E Present perfect / simple present / simple past (negatives) → Grammar 1, 3, 4

Look again at the quick facts about Nadine and say if the sentences below are true (T) or false (F). Correct the false sentences.

1 Nadine has been Ben's girlfriend for three years.
   False! She hasn't … . She …
2 She moved to the States last year.
3 Her dad works in a hospital in St. Louis.
4 Her mum has been a nurse for six months.
5 Nadine is on a sports and leisure course.
6 She doesn't like Ben very much.
7 Nadine became a student on her course two years ago.

Check-in | Training | **More please!** | Check-out

 A1.22

F Present perfect / simple present / simple past → Grammar 1, 3, 4

The world skateboarding championship is in Germany next week. Here is an interview with Andy Lewis, the world champion at the moment. Read the interview and do task 1 or 2 below.

Interviewer	Hi Andy and thanks for this interview.
Andy	No problem.
Interviewer	OK, first some questions about you. How old are you and where were you born?
Andy	I'm 21 and I was born in Boston, Massachusetts, in the USA.
Interviewer	When did you start skateboarding?
Andy	When I was a junior at high school, when I was 12.
Interviewer	Did you know then that you wanted to be a professional skateboarder?
Andy	No, not at first. It was just fun. But then when I was about 16, I took part in a competition and I won. I thought: "This is great! I can earn money like this!"
Interviewer	When did you become a pro?
Andy	After high school, when I was 18, I left Boston and moved to California. I became a pro then.
Interviewer	How long have you been world champion?
Andy	For two years now. I won my first world championship in Japan two years ago.
Interviewer	How often do you train?
Andy	I usually train about six hours every day.
Interviewer	Wow! That's a lot!
Andy	Sure, but if you want to be world champion, you have to work hard!

P ▲ **1** Write six sentences about Andy. Use the *simple present* in two sentences, the *simple past* in two and the *present perfect* in the last two:

Andy is the world champion at the moment. (simple present).
He started … (simple past) He has … (present perfect).

P ▲ **2** You are a journalist and this is your interview with Andy. Write a short article about him (100 words). Find a good headline for your article.

M ▲ **G Key words**

Look at the key words at the bottom of pages 81–85 and translate the sentences below into English.

1 Sie haben ihre eigene Firma.
2 Wenn du einen Job hast, verdienst du Geld – das ist klasse!
3 Zur Zeit hat sie keinen Job - sie ist arbeitslos.
4 Er ist seit 10 Jahren ein erfolgreicher Sänger.
5 Bitte fügen Sie in das Formular Name und Adresse ein.

5 Now you

A Work with a partner. You are two college students who are chatting online. One of you is from another country – England, the USA etc. This is your first chat so you want to find out about each other. Think of screen names for yourselves. First, complete the sentences below, then continue your chat. Use your own ideas.

Partner A (You live e.g. in the States.) What town do you live in Germany?
Partner B I live in … What about you? Where do you live?
Partner A I …
Partner B How long have you lived there?
Partner A I have … What about you? How long …?
Partner B …

B Work in small groups. Choose one of the tasks below and give a short talk to the class.

1 Did you, your family or someone you know move to Germany from another country? When? What happened?
How long have you lived in Germany now? What are your ideas about Germany?
2 Do you know a success story? It can be a famous person, someone in your family, someone you know or a friend. Tell the story.

Video Lounge Introducing people

In Unit 5 you met Jasmine, Ms Kennedy's PA. This is Ms Kennedy. She is now in her office. Jasmine is introducing Ms Kennedy to the two visitors, Mr Carter and Mr Rogers.
Watch the video. Write down the missing words from these phrases. Then make a small group. Try the conversation yourselves.

1 I'd like to … John Carter and Paul Rogers.
2 … to meet you!
3 Please, … me Diane.
4 This is my … Paul Rogers.
5 (Diane) I'm … I'm late.
6 (John) Oh, don't …
Jasmine took care of us.
7 Please have a …
(= please sit down).

Unit 6 Success stories

Check-in | Training | More please! | Check-out

6 Go for it!

P **A** The top article in the magazine today is about heroes. Do you have a 'hero'? Who is it? Tell the class.

Go for it!

college   careers   lifestyle   tech   entertainment   advice

Who is your hero?

R **B** Read the first part of the magazine article on the next page. (What is a hero?). Finish these sentences with information from the text.

1 Characters like Superman are not really heroes because …
2 A man can be a 'hero' but a woman is called a '…'
3 We often say that people we admire are heroes, people like …
4 The writer of the article thinks that the most important heroes are people who do something … or who do something …
5 Some of these people are famous but many …
6 A hero or heroine can even be …

R **C** Read the second part of the article (Stories of some real-life heroes and heroines).

1 Which person or people is this?
   a They rescued a girl from under a car.
   b He saved a man's life at a subway station.
   c They help thousand of poor people around the world.
   d She helped a woman when a man wanted to kill her.

2 Here are some reasons why people are heroes or heroines. Which reasons do you think help to describe the people in the stories in the article?
   a Heroes/Heroines don't think of themselves. They think of other people.
   b Heroes/Heroines are brave. They even risk their own life to help others.
   c Many people want to help but they don't. Heroes/Heroines act when others just think about acting.

P **D** Write a message to the *Go for it!*-magazine about your hero or heroine. Use the phrases below to help you.

Dear Go for it!
My hero/heroine is …
She/He is/was …
She/He … (What does this person do now or what did this person do in the past?)
She/He is my hero/heroine because …

Go for it!

college careers **lifestyle** tech entertainment advice

Who is your hero?

What is a hero?
Superman, Lara Croft, Wonder Woman, Iron Man. These are all superheroes and we love their films, comics and video games. But they are not real people. What is a real hero?

A hero – or 'heroine' if she is female – can just be a person who we admire. It can be a sportsperson, a film star, a politician, musician or scientist. People say:'My hero is Usain Bolt,' or 'My heroine is J.K. Rowling, the author of the Harry Potter stories.' These people do something brilliant, and they work very hard to be the best. But is that also really being a 'hero' (or 'heroine')?

Perhaps a hero or heroine is a person who does something very brave. Or who does something which helps the lives of others. Some of these heroes and heroines can become famous but often, they are just ordinary people who do something extraordinary – something 'heroic'. They may even be someone you know like a friend or a person in your family. We call people like this 'real-life heroes' and you can find them everywhere.

STORIES OF SOME REAL-LIFE HEROES AND HEROINES

One Day's Wages
American couple Eugene and Minhee Cho loved travelling but soon saw that many people around the world are terribly poor. At home, they left their jobs and started an organisation called *One Day's Wages*, which asks people to give just the money they earn in one day. Since then, they have paid for over 40 projects around the world and have saved thousands of lives.

Jumping in front of a subway train
Wesley Autrey was on the platform of a subway station in New York when a young man fell unconscious on to the railway lines. Other people looked, but Autrey jumped down to help the man. Suddenly, a train came round the corner. Autrey held the man on the ground so that the train went over them. Both lived.

Let me in!
Jenna Persia, an American teenager, was at home alone when there was a loud banging on her door. She opened it and found a woman with blood on her face. She said a man wanted to kill her. Jenna pulled the woman inside and locked the door. The man started hitting the door and shouted: 'Let me in or I'll kill you!' Jenna called the police who came and arrested the man. She saved the woman's life because she was so brave.

The world's best baseball team
A mother was in her car outside Sacramento High School to pick up her daughter. Unfortunately, she drove backwards and didn't see her daughter behind the car. The girl was trapped under the car and the mother started to scream for help. The high school baseball team heard her screams and ran to the car. Together, they picked the car up and their coach pulled the girl from under the car. He said his team were 'the world's best baseball team'.

Unit 7
Looking ahead

Check-in | Training | More please! | Check-out

1 Four American students look ahead

R, P **A** Maddy and her friend Isabella are college students in the U.S. They're answering questions in an online survey called: How do you see your life in 10 years? What are the girls' answers?

1 Do they think they'll be married in ten years?
2 Do they think they'll have a good job?
3 Do they think they'll still live in the town where they live now?

They think . . .   They don't think . . .   They don't . . .

P **B** What about YOU? Do you think you'll be married in ten years from now? Will you have a good job? What about your town or city?

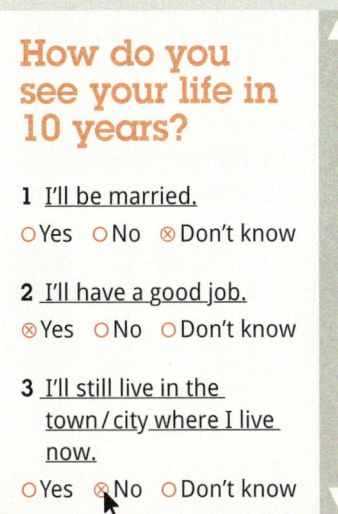

How do you see your life in 10 years?

1 I'll be married.
○ Yes   ○ No   ⊗ Don't know

2 I'll have a good job.
⊗ Yes   ○ No   ○ Don't know

3 I'll still live in the town / city where I live now.
○ Yes   ⊗ No   ○ Don't know

R **C** Brad and Wesley are college friends, too. They are talking about their next summer vacation. Read the conversation. Who's this?

Brad   **Wesley**

Do you have plans for the summer?
            Im going to look for my own apartment.
You're going to leave home?
            Yes, well, Mom and Dad are OK, but . . .
I understand. Where are you going to look?
            I'm not sure. Maybe in Highbury.
            The apartments are cheap there.
            What about you? What are you going to do?
I'm going to look for a summer job. I need some money!

1 He's going to look for a summer job.
2 He isn't going to look for a summer job.
3 He's going to leave home.
4 He's going to look for his own apartment.
5 He needs some money.

→ apartment (AE)   → summer vacation (AE)   → to leave home
→ survey   → still   → in 10 years

Am Ende von Unit 7 kann ich:
— über mein Leben in der Zukunft reden und schreiben,
— über meine Pläne für die Zukunft reden und schreiben.

Check-in | **Training** | More please! | Check-out

2 What will be different?

R **A Read about Zack and answer the questions below.**

Zack lives in Denton, a town 35 miles north of Dallas, Texas. He lives with his family and he's a student at a community college in Denton. But next September Zack's life will be very different. He'll start his first job then. In September, he'll be a receptionist in a big hotel in Dallas. He'll work at the hotel and he'll live there, too. He'll have a room at the hotel.

1 Where does Zack live now?
2 Does he have an apartment?
3 Does he have a job now?
4 What will Zack do next September?
5 What will his job be then?

P **B How will Zack's life be different next September? Make sentences like this.**

Zack is a student now. But he won't be a student next September. He'll be a hotel receptionist.
Zack ... now. But ... He ...

P **C Zack's two college friends Jay and Hunter will also start their first job next September. But what job will they have? What will they do? Work with a partner and find out.**

Partner B: Please look at page 105 now.
Partner A: You have information on the next page about Jay. Answer your partner's questions. Then ask questions and find the missing information about Hunter.

───────
→ north of   → to be different

What job will Hunter have?
When will he work?
How much will he earn?

Name	Jay Rishi
Job?	He'll be a journalist.
Where?	He'll work at a newspaper in Denton.
Live?	in an apartment in Denton
Do?	He'll interview people and he'll write articles for the paper.
Wages?	He'll earn $500 a week.
Hours?	Monday–Friday, 10 a.m. to 6.30 p.m.
Ideas about work?	He thinks he'll be a bit nervous at first. But the best thing is he'll earn his own money.

Name	Hunter Glenn
Job?	?
Where?	?
Live?	?
Do?	?
Wages?	?
Hours?	?
Ideas about work?	?

P **D** Write a short text about Jay or Hunter. Start like this:

(Jay) is a student now but next September his life will be very different. He won't be a student, he'll be a **...**

I **E** Talk in class.

What are your ideas about work? Do you think you will be nervous about your first job? Will it be interesting? Hard? What will be the best (and worst!) things about work?

P **F** Can you give the missing forms?

Will ('ll) und won't		→ More please **A – B**
I'll	I won't	
he'll	he ?	
?	she won't	live
it'll	it won't	work
we'll	?	be
?	you won't	
they'll	?	

→ wages   → to earn ($500) a week   → nervous

Unit 7 Looking ahead   **95**

Check-in | **Training** | More please! | Check-out

3 Plans for an apartment

R, P   **A**   Erin is from Florida. Last month, she got her first job and now she has her first small studio apartment. You can see a diagram of it on page 97. What is Erin going to do with the apartment? First, match the words and the pictures A – P, then listen and do task B below.

bed · bedside cabinet · coffee table · computer desk · dining table and chairs · electric kettle · houseplant · lamp · microwave · mirror · pinboard · rug · sofa · toaster · TV on a wall bracket · wall clock

R A 1.23   **B**   Listen to Erin and look at the diagram of her apartment. Note down a, b, c or d.

1. Erin is going to paint the walls of the apartment …
   - a blue
   - b white
   - c green
   - d red

2. She's going to think of the apartment as a sleeping area, a cooking area, a dining area and a … area.
   - a washing
   - b working
   - c relaxing
   - d living

3. On the wall in the sleeping area she's going to put …
   - a a mirror
   - b a clock
   - c a pinboard
   - d a TV

4. She's going to have … in the eating area.
   - a a houseplant
   - b a lamp
   - c some photos
   - d a mirror

5. In the last area where the rug is, she's going to have a sofa and …
   - a a clock
   - b a coffee table
   - c some chairs
   - d a lamp

6. Erin isn't sure yet where's she's going to put her …
   - a pinboard
   - b TV
   - c coffee table
   - d computer desk

→ studio apartment (AE > BE studio flat)   → to paint sth (white)
→ area   → (to be) sure

P, I **C Now you**

1 Work alone or in a small group.
2 Imagine that you have a new flat like Erin's. Use the diagram below and plan what you are going to do with the apartment – for example, are you going to paint the walls (if so, what colour)? What furniture and other things are you going to put in the flat (where)? Use the ideas on page 96 but think of other things, too (use your dictionary if necessary).
3 Present your ideas to the class. You could make a poster or use a projector to show your flat.

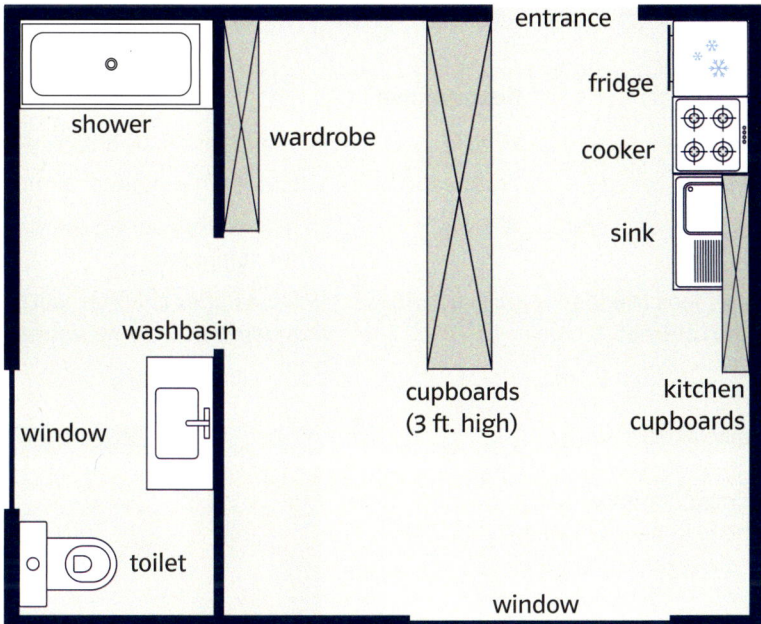

I'm / We're going to paint the walls (green / white / …).

In the living / sleeping / eating area …

I'm / We're going to put / have …

P **D Can you give the missing forms?**

Going to		→ More please **C – F**
I'm	I'm not	
?	he isn't	
she's	?	
it's	it isn't	**going to (do something)**
we're	?	
you're	?	
?	they aren't	

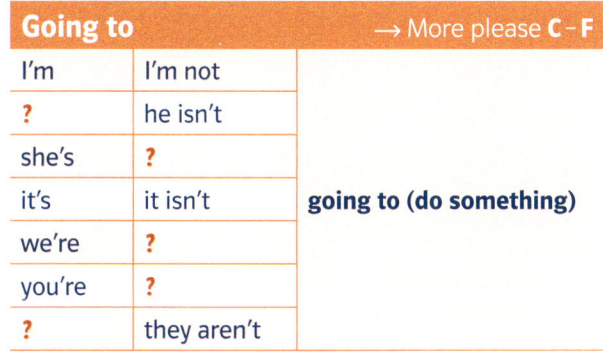

→ shower → washbasin → wardrobe → cupboard(s) → fridge
→ cooker → sink

Unit 7 Looking ahead

Check-in | Training | **More please!** | Check-out

4 More please!

R, P **A Das Futur: will** → Grammar 6

Look at the information about Nadine and answer the questions below in full sentences.

New York

Name: Nadine Frank			
Now		**Next summer**	
Where?	Göttingen, Germany	Where?	New York State, USA (6 weeks)
Occupation?	Student, vocational college	Occupation?	Volunteer in a summer camp
Lives?	At home with mum, dad, and two brothers	Will live?	In a dormitory on the camp with other volunteers
Daily activities?	Goes to college, sees friends, swims, uses the internet	Daily activities?	Will look after children, will be a lifeguard at the camp swimming pool

1. In what city does Nadine normally live?
   She normally lives in …
2. Where will she be for six weeks next summer?
3. What is her occupation when she is in her own country?
4. What will be her occupation for six weeks next year?
5. Where does Nadine normally live?
6. Will she live there next summer?
   No, she won't … – she will …
7. What sorts of things does Nadine usually do every day in her own country?
8. What sorts of things will she do every day for six weeks next summer?
9. Will she go to college for those six weeks?
10. Will she see her friends then?

R, P **B Das Futur: will** → Grammar 6

In task A above you can see some information about a young German person called Nadine Frank. Write a short text (80–100 words) about Nadine. Compare her life normally at home in Germany and her life for six weeks next summer. Begin like this:

*Nadine Frank comes from Germany. She normally lives in …
but next summer, for six weeks, she will …*

Paige   Joshua   Kayla   Michael   Amber

R, P ▲ **C Das Futur: *Going to*** → Grammar 7

These American college students are talking about their plans after college.

1 Look at the clues about each person below and match the students and the plans.
2 Write a sentences about each person.
Paige wants to … and after college she's going to …

Paige > wants to visit other countries.
Joshua > wants to work with computers.
Kayla > wants to work in the film industry.
Michael > wants to have a career in business.
Amber > wants to help young people.

R, P ▲ **D Das Futur: *Going to*** → Grammar 7

Above in task C you can see some information about five American college students.

1 Look at the clues about each person and match the students and the plans.
2 Imagine that you are interviewing the students – maybe for a college magazine. Write an interview with at least three of the students. There are some phrases below to help you.

(Name), can I begin with you?
What do you want to do after college / when you finish college / when you finish here?
So, what are your plans?
So, do you have any plans yet?
What about you, (name)? What do you want to do?
What are your …?

going to …

After college, I'm going to look for work with a marketing company.

After college, I'm going to take six months out and travel around Europe.

When I finish my course, I'm going to look for a job as a social worker.

When I finish my course, I'm going to look for a job in IT – maybe in Europe.

When I finish here, I'm going to try to get a job with a movie company.

Unit 7 Looking ahead **99**

Check-in | Training | **More please!** | **Check-out**

E Das Futur: *Going to* und *will* → Grammar 6, 7

Going to or *will*? In the pairs of sentences below, you can complete one sentence with *going to* and the other with *will* – but which is which?

1. a I have a new job! From next September I *will be* (to be) a car mechanic.
   b That means I'll have some money at last! With my wages I ... (to buy) a better car.
2. a I heard on the radio that the weather ... (to be) nice at the weekend.
   b I ... (to go) for a long bike ride in the country.
3. a Amy ... (to be) 21 next Wednesday.
   b We ... (to organise) a birthday party for her.
4. a After college, I ... (to visit) my friend in America.
   b It ... (to be) my first visit to the States and I think it ... (to be) really fascinating.
5. a ... (you / to see) the new Bond film?
   b I'm not sure. Lots of people say it ... (to be) rubbish.

Tips and tricks
Denke daran!
Du verwendest *will*, um über Fakten in der Zukunft zu sprechen und zu sagen, was voraussichtlich in der Zukunft geschehen wird – oder nicht. *Going to* verwendest du, wenn du über deine Pläne sprichst, über die Dinge, die du in der Zukunft vorhast.

F Das Futur: *Going to* und *will* → Grammar 6, 7

Going to or *will*? Complete the sentences below with the correct forms of the verbs.

1. I think people's lives in the future *will be* (to be) better than they are now.
2. When I first start work, I ... (not / to have) a lot of money.
3. We ... (to be) very busy during our business trip to London next month, but we ... (to have) one free afternoon.
4. We ... (to try) to see some of the city's famous sights on our free afternoon.
5. I have a sister in Canada. I ... (to visit) her next year.
6. I really love my boyfriend. We ... (to get) a flat together as soon as we can.
7. I think I ... (to be) quite nervous on my first day at work.

G Key words

Complete the sentences with words and phrases from the bottom of pages 93–97.

1. In Britain it's called a 'flat' but in the USA it's an '...'.
2. And Americans say '...' instead of 'holiday'.
3. He'll ... about $2,000 a month.
4. What colour are you going to ... your flat?
5. You wash your hands in a ... but you wash dishes in the kitchen ... .
6. What do you call a cupboard where you keep clothes?
   – Oh, that's a ...

5 Now you

I, P **A** Look at page 93 again then do a survey in your class called: How do you see your life in 10 (or 5) years? Make a graph and write about the answers. Here are some ideas:

I'll be married · I'll have children · I'll often speak English
I'll still live in the town where I live now · I'll travel a lot
I'll have my own firm · I'll live with my parents ·
I'll do lots of sport · I'll still like the music I like now · …

A lot of people / Most people in the class think that they …
Not many people / Only one or two people think that they …
About half / a quarter of the people in the class think that they …
(10) people in the class think that they …
Everybody / Nobody thinks that he or she …

Video Lounge Meeting a star

R, P, I It is the three British students' last day in Hollywood. Watch the video.

1 Make small groups (2–4 people).
2 Copy the table below, then make notes in the three columns.
3 Compare your notes in your group. Add new information or correct your notes.
4 One student in your group reports to the class.

Greg and Bob Quickpayne	Maya in casting	The 3 students in the movie at the end

Check-in | Training | More please! | **Check-out**

6 Go for it!

R, P **A** Look at the magazine. What will you find in the top article today? Do you sometimes read articles like this in magazines or online? Why (not)?

Go for it!

college   careers   lifestyle   tech   entertainment   advice

Your questions about love

Love is the most amazing feeling in the world. Some people say it is the most important thing in the world. But love can also be confusing – and it can hurt. Today, our expert, Doctor Love, answers some of your emails.

The ONLINE MAGAZINE for students in Germany

R **B** Read the article on the next page. True or false?

1 *inlove123* loves a girl but she only 'likes' him.
2 Doctor Love thinks that the girl will begin to love *inlove123* if he waits.
3 *confused's* boyfriend never speaks to her.
4 Doctor love thinks that *confused* should find a new boyfriend.
5 *angrywithmyfriend* broke up with his girlfriend but now she wants to come back to him.
6 Doctor Love says that *angrywithmyfriend* shouldn't be angry with his best friend.
7 *phonegirl* isn't sure if her boyfriend wants to stay with her.
8 Doctor Love says that some boys don't phone their girlfriends and that *phonegirl* shouldn't worry too much.

P, I **C** Work with a partner or in small groups. Choose one of the activities below.

1 Choose one of the emails and answers in the article. Imagine that you are the reader and write a conversation with a friend about the problem. The friend can give advice like Doctor Love's. You can begin like this:

Hi (name). How are you today?
Not too good.
Oh, what's the matter?
Well, it's my boyfriend / this girl in my class / …

2 Imagine a new 'love problem'. Write an email to the magazine about the problem and then write Doctor Love's answer.

Go for it!

college   careers   lifestyle   tech   entertainment   **advice**

Your questions about love

Love is the most amazing feeling in the world. Some people say it is the most important thing in the world. But love can also be confusing – and it can hurt. Today, our expert, Doctor Love, answers some of your emails.

Question: I love a girl in my class at college. I think about her all the time and at night I dream about her. When we meet, she is is very nice and she says she likes me. But it is clear that she doesn't have the same feelings as me. How can I make her love me?

inlove123

Doctor Love answers: I'm afraid the answer is simple – you can't make somebody love you. If this girl doesn't have feelings for you, there is nothing that you can do or say that will change that. People sometimes think that if they can change themselves – become a different person – then the person they love will suddenly fall in love with them. That isn't love. Someone must love you as you are now. If you try to change, it is sure to be a disaster in the future. Forget this girl and find another girl who has the same feelings for you. It will happen!

Question: I have gone out with my boyfriend for two months. He is lovely when we are together in private but when he is with his friends he doesn't speak to me. What is happening?

confused

Doctor Love answers: If a guy really likes you, he doesn't do this. OK, perhaps he is shy, or maybe his friends don't like you and think your boyfriend should not be with you. But I'm afraid your boyfriend must 'grow up'. Find a better boyfriend who is happy to be with you all the time.

Question: I broke up with my girlfriend two months ago. I still have feelings for her and often think about trying to get her back but now my so-called best friend is going out with her! What should I do?

angrywithmyfriend

Doctor Love answers: There is nothing that you can do. It is hard when your best friend goes out with your ex-girlfriend, but he is not wrong to do that. You broke up with her, so she was single and your friend was single, too. Did your friend know that you still have feelings for your ex-girlfriend? Probably not. It's sad, but when a relationship is over, it is over. You have to move on.

Question: When I first went out with my boyfriend he phoned me a lot. Now he never phones. He says he likes me and doesn't want to break up but I don't know what to believe.

phonegirl

Doctor Love answers: I don't think you should worry. Some guys are like that. They just don't like talking on the phone. However, talk to him about this. If he really isn't so interested in you now, you need to know.

Partner files
Job pages
Test

PARTNER FILES

Unit 4 [5 Now you]

A Ask your partner questions to find the missing facts in this article. Then answer your partner's questions.

The man's name is **(1)** _..._ He invented the modern mobile phone. He tested it for the first time on 3 April 1973. On that day, he made the first phone call in New York. **(2)** _..._ years later, the **(3)** _..._ company produced the first commercial mobile phones – mobile phones that everyone could buy. They didn't have text messaging or cameras. They weighed over **(4)** _..._! And in today's money they cost around $4,000.

Unit 7 [2 What will be different?]

C Zack's two college friends Jay and Hunter will also start their first job next September. But what job will they have? What will they do? Work with a partner and find out.

Partner B: You have information below about Hunter. Ask your partner questions and find the missing information about Jay. Then answer your partner's questions.

What job will Jay have? When will he work? What does he think about work? Where will he work / live? How much will he earn?

Name	Hunter Glenn	Name	Jay Rishi
Job?	He'll be a cowboy.	Job?	?
Where?	He'll work on a ranch.	Where?	?
Live?	He'll have a room in the ranch house.	Live?	?
Do?	He'll work on the ranch, he'll look after the cattle (Vieh).	Do?	?
Wages?	He'll earn €650 a week.	Wages?	?
Hours?	In the summer, he'll often work 7 days a week from 6 a.m. to 7 or 8 p.m.	Hours?	?
Ideas about work?	He thinks that it'll be very hard at first but that it'll be very exciting.	Ideas about work?	?

Partner files | **Job pages** | Test

JOB PAGES

Asking for and giving directions

R **A** Merve Yilmaz, from Germany, is in England. She has an interview for an internship – a 'Praktikum' – in an English company. Right now, Merve is at the railway station in the English town. She is asking for directions to the English company's offices. Read the dialogue below and look at the map of the town on page 107. In which street are the offices?

Merve   Woman in the street
Excuse me. I'm looking for this address.
    Let me see. OK. Go along here then turn right. That's High Street. Go straight up there, past the Market place, then past the post office, then turn left. That's the street you are looking for.
Great. Thanks very much. Is it far?
    No, only about ten minutes.
Thanks again.
    Not at all.

R **B** Next day, Merve is in town again. She is in front of the Mill Hotel in Victoria Street and she's asking for more directions. Read the dialogues and say which places in town she is asking about.

Merve   Passer-by
Excuse me. I'm looking for …
    Mmm, OK. Go straight up here, past the railway station, and turn left. That's Canal Street. Go up there and take the third left. The … is the first big building on your left. You can't miss it.
Thanks very much.
    You're welcome.

Merve   Passer-by
Excuse me. Is there a … near here?
    Sure. Go up here and turn right into Silver Street. Go straight up there and take the second turning on the right. The … is on your left. You can't miss it.
Thanks a lot!
    Not at all.

P, I **C** Now YOU. Work with a partner. Use the phrases below and the map to ask for and give directions to places in the town. Decide first where you both are when one of you asks for directions!

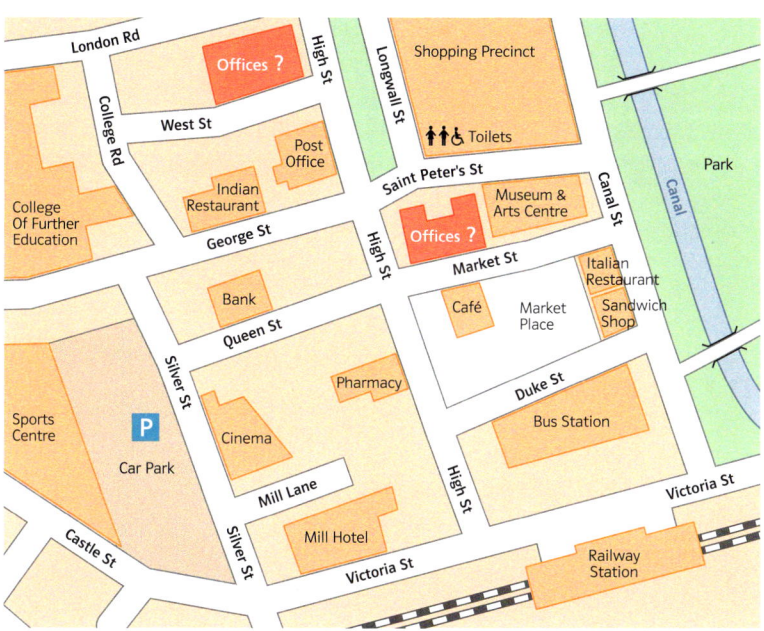

Asking for directions		
Excuse me.		
How do I	get to	the market place?
Can you tell me	the way to	
I'm looking for		the railway station.
Is there a	bank	(near) here?
Giving directions		
Go	along / (straight) up	here / High Street.
Turn	left / right.	
Take the	first / second (turning on the) left / right.	
Go	past	the post office.
Cross	over	the street.
It's	on the left / the right / opposite / next to / on the corner of …	
You can't miss it!		

Job pages 107

Partner files | **Job pages** | Test

Getting through on the phone

People use the phone all the time at work and even if you work in Germany, many phone calls today are in English. Dominik Hamann is a German businessman. He is at the airport in Germany on his way to London on a business trip. He is calling three business contacts in England before he flies.

R, P
A 1.24

A Here is the list of people who Mr Hamann wants to speak to and their companies. Listen to the three conversations. What happens? Can he speak to the people or is there perhaps a problem?

1 David James — TechArt Web Design Ltd
2 Liz Williams — Premier Advertising UK Ltd
3 Pete Marsh — Hobart Logistics

R, P **B** Now listen again to the three conversations and note down the missing words and phrases.

Conversation 1

Receptionist   **Hamann**   **James**
TechArt Web Design. Good morning.
                    Good morning. **(1)** ... David James, please?
Who is calling please?
                    It's Dominik Hamann from HB Exports in Germany.
(2) ... Mr Hamann, I'm putting you through now.
                                  Dominik, hi. How are you?
                    Hi, David. **(3)** ... . I'm at the airport in Germany. I just wanted to give you a quick call before I arrive in England ...

108

Conversation 2

Receptionist   Hamann

Premier Advertising, Craig Lewis speaking. **(4)** ... ?
　　　Hello. Can I speak to Liz Williams, please. This is Dominik Hamann from HB Exports in Germany.
I'm sorry, Mr Hamann, Liz is **(5)** ... at the moment. Will you hold?
　　　Sure. Thanks.

Conversation 3

Receptionist   Hamann

Hobart Logistics. Good morning. Sally speaking.
　　　Good morning. Can I speak to Pete Marsh, please?
I'm sorry but Mr Marsh **(6)** ... at the moment. He should be back in about half an hour. Will you call back or can he call you?
　　　I'll call back later, thanks.
Can I take **(7)** ... , please?
　　　Yes, it's Dominik Hamann from HB Exports in Germany.
Thanks, Mr Hamann. I'll tell Mr Marsh **(8)** ...
　　　Thanks. Bye now.
Goodbye.

C Now YOU. Work in small groups to make your own conversations.

1. Copy and complete the diagram below with the key phrases from the three conversations. Compare your diagrams in class. Make sure you know the German meanings of all the phrases (you can make a list of English and German phrases side by side).
2. In your group, choose two of the conversations above and write your own. Invent names, company names, etc. yourselves.
3. Read your conversations to the class – or record them and play the recordings.

Receptionist: Good morning ...
Caller:　　　Could I speak to ...

Receptionist: One moment ...   **Receptionist:** I'm sorry ...   **Receptionist:** I'm sorry ...
...   .

job pages   109

Partner files | **Job pages** | Test

Can I take a message?

Monja Jekewitz works for an American multinational company in Germany. She is a personal assistant to Ms Baker, the firm's marketing manager in Germany. In her job, Monja answers Ms Baker's phone and often puts callers through to her boss. This week, however, Ms Baker is on holiday, and Monja is taking messages when people ring.

R, P **A** Read the telephone conversation and complete Monja's message with the missing information.

Monja   Mr Kessler

Monja Jekewitz.
         Morning, Monja. It's Alan Kessler from the New York office. Can I speak to Ms Baker, please?
Good morning, Mr Kessler. I'm afraid Ms Baker isn't here this week. Can I take a message?
         Yes. Can you tell her I'm coming to Germany in two week's time and that I'd like to meet her if she has time? The best day for me would be Thursday March 24.
I'll just repeat that. You're coming to Germany in two week's time and you'd like to meet Ms Baker. The best day for you would be March 24.
         That's right. Thanks, Monja.
You're welcome, Mr Kessler. I'll give Ms Baker your message as soon as she's back.

TELEPHONE MESSAGE

DATE: 9 March
FROM: Mr Kessler, New York office

Mr Kessler is coming to Germany in (1) … week's time and would like to meet you. The best day for him would be (2) …

B Monja is having another conversation on the phone. Complete the conversation with suitable phrases from the 'Leaving and taking messages' box below the conversation. Then copy and complete the telephone message for Ms Baker.

Monja   Mr Carter

Monja Jekewitz.
  Good morning, Monja. It's Bill Carter from the advertising agency in London. Can I speak to Ms Baker, please?
Good morning, Mr Carter. **(1)** ... Ms Baker isn't here this week. **(2)** ... ?
  Yes. **(3)** ... I'm really sorry but I can't make the meeting with her on the 30th of March. I'll call her one day next week to fix another time.
I'll just repeat that. You **(4)** ... .
  That's right. Thanks, Monja.
You're welcome, Mr Carter. **(5)** ... Ms Baker your message as soon as she's back.

Leaving and taking messages			
Secretary	I'm afraid I'm sorry but	Mr / Mrs / Ms X	isn't here at the moment. isn't in the office today. is away / on holiday this week.
	Can I Would you like to	take a message? leave a message?	
Caller	Can you tell	her / him / Mr / Mrs / Ms ...	(that) **I am coming** ...?
Secretary	I'll just Can I just	repeat that. repeat that?	
	You	**are coming ...**	
Message	**Mr / Mrs / Ms ...**	**is coming ...**	
Caller	That's right. Thanks very much.		
Secretary	You're welcome.		
	I'll give	Mr / Mrs / Ms ...	your message as soon as (s)he is back.

TELEPHONE MESSAGE

DATE: 10 March
FROM: Mr Carter, advertising agency, London

Mr Carter is sorry but he ...

C Now YOU. You will hear two phone conversations between Monja and people who would like to speak to Ms Baker this week. They are Mr Ramirez and Ms Fisher. Prepare some message forms, listen to the conversations, and write the messages. The date for both calls is 11 March.

Partner files | **Job pages** | Test

Ceyda   Dominik and Verena

Emails at work

In today's world, everybody uses emails at work. Dominik works for a big German construction firm. He often works on projects with people from other countries. Verena works in a German hairdressing salon but the salon buys lots of products from the UK and the USA. And Ceyda works for a German media company. She writes every day to people around the world. Below you can see three of their emails. Look at them now and do the tasks on page 113.

To: p.smith@londonarchitects.co.uk
Subject: building plans

Hi Paul
Could you please send me a copy of the plans for the next phase of the building? Thanks in advance!
Best wishes
Dominik

To: dave.edwards@hairandbeauty.co.uk
Subject: price list

Dear Dave
Do you have a complete price list for your new hair colour products? We like them very much!
Kind regards
Verena

To: m.lieberman@nyarts.com
Subject: film festival dates

Hey Molly
Hope you're well. Could you please send me the dates of next year's New York Film Festival? Many thanks!
Ceyda

R, P **A** Below are the replies that Dominik, Verena and Ceyda got to their emails – but they are not in the right order. Match the replies and the emails, then write out the replies below in full.

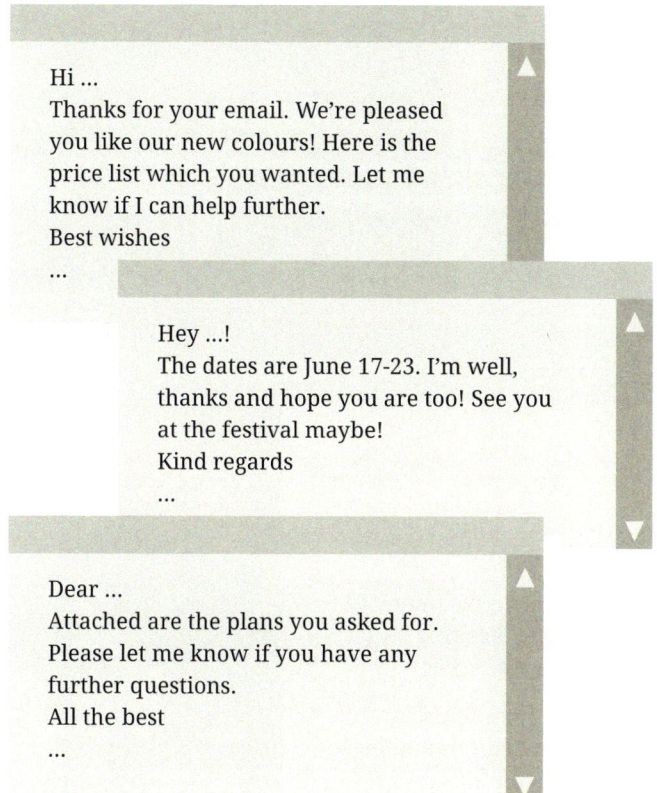

> Hi ...
> Thanks for your email. We're pleased you like our new colours! Here is the price list which you wanted. Let me know if I can help further.
> Best wishes
> ...

> Hey ...!
> The dates are June 17-23. I'm well, thanks and hope you are too! See you at the festival maybe!
> Kind regards
> ...

> Dear ...
> Attached are the plans you asked for. Please let me know if you have any further questions.
> All the best
> ...

Hier und dort

In Großbritannien und in den USA sind E-Mails auf der Arbeit oft kurz und umgangssprachlich. Die Kollegen, die regelmäßig miteinander korrespondieren, sprechen sich für gewöhnlich mit ihren Vornamen an. Allerdings ist die Sprache trotzdem höflich, also achte darauf, dass du *please* und *thank you* sagst und höfliche Ausdrücke wie *Could you ...?* verwendest.

M, I **B** Here are some phrases that you often use in emails at work. Work with a partner. Copy and complete the table with German translations. Compare your answers in class.

Beginning your email		Replying	
Dear / Hi / Hey	Liebe/r/...	Here is / are the ... which you wanted	Hier ist / sind ...
Hope you're well		Attached is / are ...	
Could you please send me ...?		(Please) let me know if you have any further questions / if I can help further	
Do you have ...?		Best wishes / Kind regards	
Many thanks / Thanks in advance		All the best	

R, P, I **C** Now YOU! In class, brainstorm some ideas for emails at work – use the emails above as models. Then in groups, write emails. Exchange these with another group and write replies to their emails. Think of dates, times, names etc. yourselves.

Partner files | Job pages | **Test**

TEST

1 Reading

You find the article below online. Read the text and do the tasks on page 115.

Fishing in Alaska is a cold, hard job!

There are many different jobs in America from shop assistants to circus clowns, but what are the most dangerous – which workers have the kinds of jobs where it is possible that they may die? In this article, we look at …

America's most dangerous jobs!

Police officers and firefighters have dangerous jobs. We see them on TV or in movies. Their jobs are famous – maybe even 'exciting'. But, in fact, they aren't the most dangerous jobs in America today.

The number one dangerous job in the USA today is a timber cutter. These people work high in the air with dangerous machines and big trees. Most die or are badly injured when trees fall on them. Every year, per every 100,000 timber workers, 120 die.

The number two most dangerous job is a fisher. Fishing is always dangerous but in the far north of the USA, in Alaska, in winter, it can be a really terrible job. Alaskan fishers catch crabs in winter. They work hundreds of kilometres from land, in storms, ice and snow. The temperature can sometimes be 40 degrees below freezing. And they often work 40 hours in every 50 hours. It is perhaps not surprising, therefore, that around 70 fishers die every year per 100,000 workers.

Another dangerous job is that of a steel worker. You have maybe seen them at work on tall buildings like skyscrapers. Clearly, these people work high in the air every day and there is always the possibility that they can fall. In fact, per 100,000 steel workers, 60 die every year – most because they fall. This really is a job for people who are young and physically very fit.

The big airliners we fly in when we go on holiday are very safe and passengers never die. But every year in the USA, around 70 pilots die in small planes. One of the most dangerous jobs for a pilot is to be a crop sprayer. When they are spraying crops, pilots must fast

America's **most dangerous** job? A timber cutter.

Some pilots fly small planes like this one. They **spray crops** to protect them against insects and diseases

< left: A steel worker at work on a **skyscraper**
> right: Around 25 truck drivers per 100,000 die every year on America's highways

and very, very low. They know that if they make one mistake, they will crash and that the crash can kill them.

Finally, the other most dangerous jobs in America are on the roads. Traffic is always dangerous. In New York, cycle couriers deliver thousands of letters and packages every day to offices in the city. They have to work fast and they often hold cars and trucks with their hands so that they can go faster. Lots of them die or have bad accidents. But the most dangerous job on the roads is to be a truck driver. Every year, around 25 per 100,000 die in an accident. Most of the time this happens when drivers work too long hours. They become tired and then they fall asleep on the road. The result is almost always a bad accident or death.

A Decide whether the sentences below are true or false according to the text. Write down T or F.

1 Police officers and firefighters have the most dangerous jobs in the USA.
2 The people who build skyscrapers are called steel workers.
3 Small planes are safe but big airliners are dangerous.
4 Cycle couriers in New York often travel in cars or trucks.
5 Per 100,000 truck drivers, around 25 die every year in accidents.

B Choose the correct answer. Write down a, b or c.

1 Alaskan fishers often work …
   a high in the air.   b very long hours.   c in small ships.

2 The reason why truck drivers often have accidents is that they …
   a fall.   b fly too low.   c don't stop to rest.

3 New York cycle couriers …
   a deliver things.   b protect people.   c always have bad accidents.

4 Most timber cutters die because of …
   a falling trees.   b dangerous machines.   c small mistakes when they fly.

5 All of the workers in this text have jobs that …
   a are exciting.   b are easy.   d can kill them.

→ per *pro*   → crab *Krebs*   → physically *körperlich*   → courier *Kurier, Eilbote*

Partner files | Job pages | **Test**

2 Listening

A 1.26

You are going to hear a recording of a young British woman called Becky. You will hear the recording twice. Listen and choose the correct answers. Write down a, b, c.

1 Becky is …
   a an office worker.   b a teacher.   c a tour guide.

2 Becky's company has existed since …
   a 1906.   b 1806.   c 1706.

3 Back then people …
   a liked coffee better than tea.
   b liked tea better than coffee.
   c didn't drink tea or coffee.

4 Thomas Turner opened his first shop …
   a in the building next door to where Becky is now.
   b in the building where Becky is now.
   c in a building in the next street to where Becky is now.

5 Tea was soon 'in' in London because …
   a Thomas Turner was a famous man.
   b Thomas Turner's tea was cheap.
   c famous people came to his tea shop.

6 1837 was an important year because …
   a Thomas Turner opened a second shop.
   b the British queen at the time started buying Turners tea.
   c the British queen at the time visited Thomas Turner's tea shop.

7 Today, Turners sells its tea in … countries around the world
   a 23   b 32   c 33

8 Becky says it's 'amazing' that …
   a Indian people drink Turners tea.
   b Americans drink Turners tea.
   c British people still like Turners tea.

9 The modern Turners company has … employees.
   a 1,200   b 3,200   c 2,300

10 Last year, the company's turnover was …
    a around $1 billion.
    b over $1 billion.
    c almost $1 billion.

11 Next, the visitors will go to …
    a Turners head office.   b a museum.   c Turners tea shop.

116

3 Mediation

A Du bist mit Freunden im Urlaub in Neuseeland. Deine Freunde sprechen kein Englisch und wollen wissen, was diese Schilder bedeuten. Erkläre sie ihnen kurz auf Deutsch.

B Now explain to an English person – in English of course – what these German signs at work mean.

4 Writing

You have a page on the social networking site *myface*. Your page is in German at the moment but you want to post it also in English. Write a text (80–100 words) about yourself in English to post online. Include all the following information:

- where you live,
- when you started being a student at your college,
- two facts about your college and your course,
- two things you like doing in your free time,
- one thing that you think (or hope) that you will do one day in the future.

Anhang
Grammar summary
Skills files
Vocabulary

GRAMMAR SUMMARY

1 Das simple present

A Allgemein

Das simple present wird verwendet:
- für Aussagen, die längere Zeit gültig sind,
- um auszudrücken, was jemand regelmäßig tut.

> I **go** to college five days a week.
>
> I **live** in Germany.

B Mit *sometimes*, *often* usw.

Da man mit dem simple present ausdrückt, was man regelmäßig tut, wird es oft mit Wörtern wie *usually*, *normally*, *sometimes*, *often*, *always*, *never* verwendet. Diese Wörter (Adverbien) stehen immer:
- **vor** einem Vollverb,
- **nach** to be.

> I **usually** get up at 7 a.m.
>
> I **often** watch TV in the evenings.
>
> I'm **always** happy on Fridays.

C Bildung: Aussagen

Das simple present wird aus der Grundform des Verbs (Infinitiv ohne *to*) gebildet. Nach *he/she/it* endet das Verb immer auf *-s* oder *-es*!

a An die meisten Verben wird einfach *-s* angehängt.
b Die Endung *-es* wird bei Verben benutzt, die auf *s*, *ss*, *x*, *ch*, oder *sh* enden (z. B. *to finish*), da es schwer wäre, nur ein *-s* auszusprechen.
c Auch *to go* und *to do* enden mit *-es*.
d Ein Sonderfall sind Verben, die auf *-y* enden: *to tidy* ⟶ *he tid**ies***.

a to work	b to finish
I work	I finish
he / she / it work**s**	he / she / it finish**es**
we work	we finish
you work	you finish
they work	they finish

c to go	d to tidy
I go	I tidy
he / she / it go**es**	he / she / it tid**ies**
we go	we tidy
you go	you tidy
they go	they tidy

D Bildung: Fragen und Verneinungen

- Fragen im simple present werden mit *do* (bei *he/she/it*: *does*) gebildet.
- Verneinungen bildet man mit *don't* (nach *he/she/it*: *doesn't*).

VORSICHT!
Nach *does/doesn't* kommt immer die Grundform des Verbs:
Does he work? (! *Does he works?*)
She doesn't work. (! *She doesn't works.*)

Fragen	Verneinungen
Do I work?	I don't work
Does he / she / it wor**k**?	he / she / it doesn't wor**k**
Do we work?	we don't work
Do you work?	you don't work
Do they work?	they don't work

Grammar summary | Skills files | Vocabulary

2 Das present continuous

A Allgemein

Das present continuous benutzt man für Aktivitäten, die gerade im Augenblick des Sprechens stattfinden. Oder auch um ein Bild zu beschreiben. Es wird häufig mit Zeitangaben wie *at the moment* und *right now* verwendet.

> I**'m reading** this text at the moment.
>
> What can you see in this photo?
> – A hairdresser. Right now, she**'s cutting** a customer's hair.

B Mit *this week*, *this month* usw.

Das present continuous kann auch für längere, befristete Handlungen verwendet werden, die gerade stattfinden, benutzt werden, z. B. *this week*, *this month*.

> We**'re visiting** some friends in England this week.
> Julia **is learning** English on a course in London.

C Bildung: Aussagen

Das present continuous wird mit *to be* und Verb + *-ing* gebildet.

I'm he's / she's / it's we're you're they're	working	I'm not working she isn't working
		Am I working? Are you working? Are they working?

D Bildung: Fragen und Verneinungen

Fragen und Verneinungen werden mit den Frage- und Verneinungsformen von *to be* gebildet.

Verb + *-ing*: Schreibregeln
- An die meisten Verben wird einfach *-ing* angehängt:
  work – working, *do – doing*.
- Verben, die auf *-e* enden, verlieren das *-e*:
  use – using, *dance – dancing*.
- Kurze Verben, die auf einen Vokal und einen Konsonanten (außer *-y*, *-w* und *-x*) enden, verdoppeln den Konsonanten:
  cut – cutting (aber *play – playing*).
- Längere Verben, die auf einen Vokal und einen Konsonanten enden, verdoppeln den Konsonanten nicht:
  visit – visiting, *deliver – delivering*.
  (Ausnahmen: *travelling*, *beginning*)
- Bei Verben, die auf *-ie* enden, wird *-ie* zu *-y*: *die – dying*

This is Patrick. He lives in England. He goes to an FE college five days a week.

It's 8.30 in the morning. Patrick is going to college by bus.

3 Das simple past

A Allgemein

Das simple past wird verwendet, um Ereignisse in der Vergangenheit zu schildern, die jetzt abgeschlossen sind. Es wird häufig mit Zeitangaben wie *then*, *in 1970*, *last week* und *30 years ago* benutzt.

B Bildung: Aussagen

- Regelmäßige Verben bilden das simple past mit *-ed*. Diese Form bleibt in allen Personen gleich.
- Unregelmäßige Verben haben Sonderformen im simple past (eine Liste findest du auf dem Klappumschlag). Diese Formen (außer bei *to be*) bleiben ebenfalls in allen Personen gleich.

regelmäßig	unregelmäßig	
to work	**to go**	**to be**
I worked	I went	I **was**
he worked	he went	he was
she worked	she went	she was
it worked	it went	it was
we worked	we went	we **were**
you worked	you went	you were
they worked	they went	they were

C Bildung: Fragen und Verneinungen

- Fragen im simple past werden in allen Personen mit *did* gebildet.
- Verneinungen bildet man durchgehend mit *didn't*.
- *to be* bildet Fragen und Verneinungen im simple past mit eigenen Formen.

VORSICHT!
Nach *did/didn't* steht immer die Grundform des Verbs:
Did he work? (**!** *Did he worked?*)
She didn't work. (**!** *She didn't worked.*)

Fragen	Verneinungen
Did I work?	I didn't work
Did he / she / it work?	he / she / it didn't work
Did we work?	we didn't work
Did you work?	you didn't work
Did they work?	they didn't work

to be	
Was I?	I wasn't
Was he / she / it?	he / she / it wasn't
Were we / you / they?	we / you / they / weren't

Verb + *-ed*: Schreibregeln
- An die meisten Verben wird einfach *-ed* angehängt: *work – work**ed***.
- An Verben, die auf *-e* enden, hangt man nur *-d* an: *us**e** – us**ed***, *danc**e** – danc**ed***.
- Kurze Verben, die auf einen Vokal *(a, e, i o, u)* und einen Konsonanten (außer *-y*, *-w* und *-x*) enden, verdoppeln den Konsonanten: *sho**p** – sho**pp**ed*, *jo**g** – jo**gg**ed*.
- Längere Verben, die auf einen Vokal und einen Konsonanten enden, verdoppeln den Konsonanten nicht:
*visi**t** – visi**t**ed*, *delive**r** – delive**r**ed*. (Ausnahme: *trave**ll**ed*)
- Bei Verben, die auf *-y* enden, wird *-y* zu *-i*: *stud**y** – stud**ied***.

4 Das present perfect

A Allgemein

How long has Julie had that electric guitar?
For about two days.

Mit dem present perfect und *since/for* kann man 'Wie lange'-Fragen *(How long …?)* beantworten.
- *Since* wird mit einem Zeitpunkt (z. B. *2001, 3 January, last year*) benutzt.
- *For* verwendet man für einen Zeitraum (z. B. *two years, six months*).

B Bildung: Aussagen

Das present perfect wird mit *to have* und der 3. Form (Partizip Perfekt) gebildet.
- Regelmäßige Verben (wie *to work*) bilden ihre 3. Form mit *-ed*.
- Unregelmäßige Verben (wie *to go*) haben Sonderformen, die in der Liste auf dem Klappumschlag zu finden sind.

I have (I've) he has (he's) she has (she's) it has (it's) we have (we've) you have (you've) they have (they've)	worked gone

C Bildung: Fragen und Verneinungen

Fragen und Verneinungen werden mit Frage- und Verneinungsformen von *to have* + 3. Form des Verbs gebildet.

Have you worked? Has he worked?
I haven't worked he/she/it hasn't worked we/you/they haven't worked

5 Die Steigerung der Adjektive

A Allgemein

Wir verwenden die Steigerungsformen von Adjektiven *(Comparative* und *Superlative)*, um Personen und Sachen miteinander zu vergleichen.

My boss is **nice**.
She's **nicer than** your boss!
She's **the nicest** boss in our office.

B Bildung

- Einsilbige Adjektive werden mit *-er/-est* gesteigert. Achte auf folgende Schreibregeln:
  – Bei Adjektiven mit *-e* am Ende entfällt das *-e*.
  – Adjektive, die auf Vokal + Konsonant enden, verdoppeln den Konsonanten.
- Alle Adjektive mit Konsonant + *-y* am Ende werden ebenfalls mit *-er/-est* gesteigert. Das *-y* wird dabei zu *-i*!
- Andere (längere) Adjektive werden mit *more* und *most* gesteigert.
- Die Adjektive *good* und *bad* haben unregelmäßige Steigerungsformen.

Adjective	Comparative	Superlative
cheap	cheap**er**	(the) cheap**est**
nice	nic**er**	(the) nic**est**
big	bi**gg**er	(the) bi**gg**est
friendly	friendl**ier**	(the) friendl**iest**
important	**more** important	(the) **most** important
good bad	**better worse**	(the) **best** (the) **worst**

6 Das Futur: *will*

A Allgemein

Will wird für feststehende Ereignisse in der Zukunft sowie für Vorhersagen und Vermutungen verwendet.

> I**'ll have** a family in 10 years.
> She **won't leave** her job when she has a family.

B Bildung

- **Aussagen** werden mit *will* + Grundform des Verbs gebildet. Die Kurzform (*'ll*) wird fast immer beim Sprechen und häufig auch beim Schreiben verwendet.
- **Fragen** bildet man, indem man *will* und das Subjekt tauscht. Hier sind die Kurzformen nicht möglich.
- **Verneinungen** werden mit *won't* + Grundform des Verbs gebildet.

I will (I'll) come	Will I come?
he will (he'll) come	Will he come?
she will (she'll) come	Will she come?
it will (it'll) come	Will it come?
we will (we'll) come	Will we come?
you will (you'll) come	Will you come?
they will (they'll) come	Will they come?

I won't come
he / she / it won't come
we / you / they won't come

7 Das Futur: *going to*

A Allgemein

Going to verwendet man, um über Pläne und Vorhaben zu sprechen: *I'm going to buy a new jacket* entspricht etwa auf Deutsch: „Ich habe vor, eine neue Jacke zu kaufen."

> I**'m going to** move to a new apartment next month.
> **Are** you **going to** leave home?

B Bildung

- **Aussagen** bildet man mit *to be* + *going to* + Hauptverb.
- **Fragen** bildet man mit den Frageformen von *to be* + *going to* + Hauptverb.
- Für **Verneinungen** benutzt man die Verneinung von *to be* + *going to* + Hauptverb.

I'm he's / she's / it's we're / you're / they're	going to	work
Am I Is he / she / it Are we / you / they	going to	work?
I'm not he / she / it isn't we / you / they aren't	going to	work

Will und *going to*

It won't rain tomorrow.

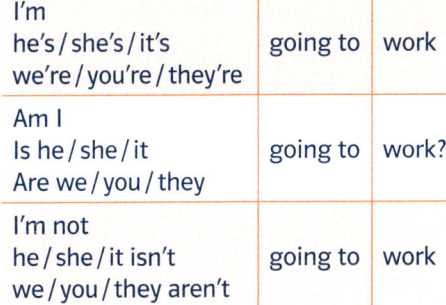

When I'm big, I'm going to be a footballer!

Grammar summary | Skills files | Vocabulary

8 Modale Hilfsverben: *must, have to, mustn't* und *don't / doesn't have to*

A Allgemein

Mit den modalen Hilfsverben *must, have to, mustn't* und *don't / doesn't have to* wird ausgedrückt, was man tun muss, nicht tun darf und nicht zu tun braucht (nicht tun muss).

- **must / have to**
  In England you must / have to drive on the left.

- **mustn't**
  You mustn't drive on the right!

- **don't / doesn't have to**
  He doesn't have to drive! He has a driver.

Must und *have to* haben etwa die gleiche Bedeutung. Sie drücken aus, was man tun **muss**.	*Mustn't* drückt aus, was man **nicht darf**. **VORSICHT!** *mustn't* bedeutet nicht ‚nicht müssen'.	*Don't / Doesn't have to* drückt aus, was man **nicht zu tun braucht**. **VORSICHT!** *don't have to* = nicht müssen

B Bildung: *must* und *have to*

- *Must* bleibt in allen Personen gleich. Auf *must* folgt die Grundform des Verbs.
- *Have to* bildet man mit *to have* + Grundform des Verbs.

must	have to
I must go he / she / it must go we / you / they must go	I have to go he / she / it has to go we / you / they have to go

C Bildung: *mustn't*

Mustn't bleibt ebenfalls bei allen Personen gleich. Auf *mustn't* folgt die Grundform des Verbs.

I mustn't he / she / it mustn't we / you / they mustn't	go

D Bildung: *don't / doesn't have to*

Die Verneinungsform von *have to* bildet man mit *don't / doesn't have to* + Grundform des Verbs.

I don't have to he / she / it doesn't have to we / you / they don't have to	go

9 *If*-Sätze (Bedingungssätze)

A Allgemein

- Ein Bedingungssatz besteht aus einem *if*-Teil und einem Hauptsatz. Der *if*-Teil beschreibt eine Bedingung und der Hauptsatz drückt aus, was passieren wird oder passieren könnte (oder hätte passieren können), wenn diese Bedingung erfüllt wird.
- Bedingungssätze können entweder mit dem *if*-Teil oder mit dem Hauptsatz beginnen. Wenn der *if*-Teil beginnt, steht immer ein Komma vor dem Hauptsatz.
- Es gibt drei Grundtypen von *if*-Sätzen: Typ 1, 2 und 3.

B *If*-Sätze Typ 1:

If you **ask** the robot, it **will clean** the house.
- Typ 1 drückt aus, was unter bestimmten Bedingungen in der Zukunft geschehen wird oder nicht geschehen wird.

If + simple present	will + Verb
If you go to the party,	you'll see Mitch.

C *If*-Sätze Typ 2:

If I **worked** for that company, I **would need** a good qualification.
- Wir benutzen Typ 2, um über eventuelle Situationen zu sprechen oder wenn du zweifelst, dass eine Bedingung erfüllbar ist.
- **VORSICHT!** Anders als im Deutschen darf *would* nur im Hauptsatz, nicht im *if*-Teil stehen.

If + simple past	would(n't) + Verb
If you went to the party,	you would see Mitch.

D *If*-Sätze Typ 3:

If he **had stayed** on the streets, he **would have died**.
- Typ 3 schildert Ereignisse in der Vergangenheit, die hätten passieren können – die aber nicht passiert sind.

If + past perfect	would(n't) have + Partizip Perfekt (3. Form)
If you had gone to the party,	you would have seen Mitch.

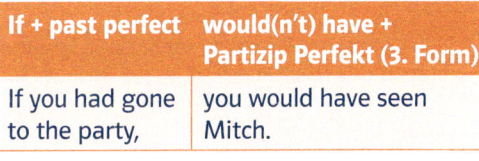

Typ 1: Für Sachen, die passieren werden, wenn …

Typ 2: Für imaginäre, schwer vorstellbare Situationen

Typ 3: Für Sachen, die hätten passieren können

10 Das Passiv

A Allgemein: Aktiv- und Passivsätze

- Aktivsätze betonen, **wer** etwas tut. Passivsätze betonen, **was** getan wird – die Handlung steht im Vordergrund.
- In *Kickoff Foundation* findest du nur **Aktivsätze**. In einem Aktivsatz steht das Subjekt vor dem Verb. Gibt es ein Objekt, so steht dieses nach dem Verb.
- **Passivsätze** kann man als ‚umgedrehte' Aktivsätze ansehen: Das Objekt des Aktivsatzes wird zum Subjekt des Passivsatzes.

Aktivsatz		
Subjekt	Verb	Objekt
The man	bought	the flowers.

Passivsatz
The man bought the flowers.
The flowers were bought by the man.

B Bildung

- Das Passiv wird mit *to be* + 3. Form des Verbs (Partizip Perfekt) gebildet.

simple present		simple past	
I'm		I was	
he's		he was	
she's		she was	
it's	**made**	it was	**made**
we're		we were	
you're		you were	
they're		they were	

C Mit oder ohne *by*?

Meist wird das Subjekt des Aktivsatzes in einem Passivsatz nicht genannt. Wollen wir aber das Subjekt besonders betonen, können wir es mit Hilfe von *by* am Satzende anfügen. In Satz **a** ist der Name des Regisseurs besonders wichtig. In Satz **b** ist es uninteressant, von wem die Blumen angebaut werden.

a *The film was made **by Steven Spielberg**.*
b *These flowers are grown in **Kenya** (by …).*

They delivered oranges to the supermarket yesterday.

Too many oranges were delivered to the supermarket yesterday!

11 Adjektive und Adverbien

A Allgemein

- **Adjektive** beschreiben Personen und Sachen. Sie stehen meist vor einem Substantiv oder nach *to be*.
- **Adverbien** sagen etwas über Verben aus. Sie sagen uns, **wie** etwas passiert

a **big** robot
The robot is **big**.

The robot loads the lorries **quickly**.

B Adverbien: Bildung

- Ein Adverb wird gebildet, indem *-ly* an das Adjektiv angehängt wird.
- Bei Adjektiven mit der Endung *-y* wird das *-y* zu *-ily*.
- Die Endung *-le* wird zu *-ly*.
- *-ic* wird zu *-ically*.
- Das Adverb von *good* ist *well*.

Adjektiv	Adverb
quick	quick**ly**
easy	eas**ily**
simple	simp**ly**
automatic	automat**ically**
good	well

12 Relativsätze

A Allgemein

Relativsätze sind Sätze, die eines der Relativpronomen *who*, *which* oder *where* enthalten. Sie beschreiben das Wort, auf das sie sich beziehen, näher.

The woman who is helping him is Frau Bliscz.
The document which she has in her hand is Herr Krueger's boarding card.

D *who*, *which* oder *where*?

- *who* für Personen
- *which* für Sachen
- *where* für Orte

A passenger is a person **who** travels by plane.
A plane is a machine **which** carries people.
The place **where** passengers check in is the check-in desk.

Boris can do things very quickly.

The guy who goes to a fitness club every day is A or B?

Grammar summary | **Skills files** | Vocabulary

SKILLS FILES

1 Einen längeren Text verstehen

Vor dem Lesen:
1. Woher kommt der Text: Zeitung? Sachbuch? Roman? … ?
2. Handelt es sich um einen Sachtext oder um einen fiktionalen Text?
3. Was erwartest du, wenn du die Bilder und den Titel ansiehst? Wird der Text sachlich, spannend, informativ, … sein?
4. Weißt du etwas über den Autor und die Zeit, in der der Text spielt bzw. geschrieben wurde?

Beim ersten Lesen:
Lies den Text. Ist er so, wie du erwartet hast? Was ist anders?

Beim zweiten Lesen:
Wie kannst du die Bedeutung der neuen Wörter erschließen?

A crazy idea!
For centuries stories about UFOs and aliens have attracted people: Spaceships land on the Earth, people go out to take photos and never **return**, aliens enter the **brains** of people and control their bodies, **hideous** creatures try to **take control of** our world. Many people all over the world believe that there are aliens on the Earth. There are thousands of stories from people who **claim** that they have seen UFOs, met aliens or been on an alien planet. But **astronomers** and other scientists are more **sceptical**. They want facts not fiction. They say that the chances of meeting an alien are not very high and most of these stories come from people who have **visions**. Others have a lot of **imagination** and believe that what they imagined really happened.

Schau dir die markierten Wörter an und lies dazu folgende Tipps:

Vergleich: Was könnte das englische Wort *return* bedeuten? Überlege, ob du ein ähnliches Wort in einer anderen Sprache kennst: z.B das französische Wort *retourner*.
Logische Ableitung: Das Wort *body* ist dir bekannt. Was könnte dann *brain* sein, wenn es deinen Körper kontrolliert?
Kontext: Ein Wort wie *hideous* kannst du nur mithilfe der Wörter erraten, die es umgeben. Ist es wohl eher ein positives Wort wie *beautiful* oder ein negatives wie *horrible*?
Wortbildung: Du kennst bereits das Nomen *control*. Was könnte der Ausdruck *take control of* bedeuten? Das Verb *imagine* ist dir auch bekannt, so dass *imagination* leicht zu verstehen ist.
Deutsch: Die fehlenden drei neuen Wörter kannst du erraten, weil sie deutschen Wörtern ähneln: z.B.: *sceptical* = skeptisch.
Das heißt, du müsstest nur das Wort *claim* im Wörterbuch nachschlagen, falls du es doch nicht aus dem Kontext heraus verstehen kannst.

Nach dem zweiten Lesen:
1. Was ist das Hauptthema: Astronomers? The Earth? Aliens?
2. Wie ist die Argumentationskette bzw. der Handlungsverlauf: Welches sind die Argumente dafür und dagegen?/Was passiert?
3. Was ist die Schlussfolgerung?/Wie endet der Text?

2 Lesetexte unterscheiden

1. Man kann Texte in zwei Hauptgruppen aufteilen: Sachtexte und fiktionale Texte.

Sachtexte / Nicht fiktionale Texte *(fact)*	Fiktionale Texte *(fiction)*
Anzeige, Zeitungsartikel, Bewerbungsbrief, Biocard, CV (Lebenslauf) usw.	Kurzgeschichte, Auszug aus einem Roman, Erzählung, Gedicht, Lied, Drama usw.

2. Die Texte in diesen Gruppen haben viele Gemeinsamkeiten, aber manches ist doch anders. Hier ein kurzer Überblick. Unten findest du zwei Beispiele. Vielleicht fallen dir noch Punkte ein.

	Eigenschaften	Sachtext	Fiktionaler Text
1	Titel	direkt und informativ	oft indirekt bzw. Wortspiel
2	Bild(er)	Diagramme, Fotos mit klaren Aussagen	Zeichnungen, Stimmungsbilder
3	Anfang	leitet das Thema ein	führt in den Handlungsrahmen ein
4	Absätze	Es wird jeweils ein neuer Sachaspekt eingeleitet bzw. vertieft.	Es wird ein Wechsel von Ort, Zeit, Personen und Handlung angezeigt.
5	Schluss	Schlussfolgerung	sehr unterschiedlich, z. B. Lösung, offenes Ende
6	Ziel des Lesens	Argumente / Infos zur Weiterbearbeitung vermitteln	Unterhaltung, Kritik äußern, Lebenserfahrungen vermitteln
7	Stil	berichtende, zumeist sachliche Sprache	erzählend, oft mit wörtlicher Rede, Fragen, Ausrufen

TAVISTOCK TIMES

(1) UFO reported – 15-year-old missing

(2)

A 15-year-old boy is missing after he went to investigate a UFO on Friday. **(3)** His parents contacted the police the next morning. They reported that their son, Darly, had not come home after he had gone out to take photos of a UFO.
(4) The pupil from a school in Tavistock was last seen on Friday night with two friends after supper. One of them phoned Darly at around 6 o'clock and said that he had seen a UFO over the moors.
(5) The three boys set off on their bikes but only two of them came home at ten o'clock. The parents are certain that their son has been taken by aliens. **(6) + (7)**

A **(1)** Sci-Fi adventure story:
How we lost Darly

(2)

I knew when I phoned Darly that night that he would go with us to the moor. **(3)**
(4) "Of course I'll come with you. I'll get my camera and meet you in ten minutes at the end of the road."
Around 7 o'clock we reached the place where we thought that the UFO had landed. It was dark and windy. Then the rain started. It got so heavy that we decided to wait under a big tree. As we were running to it, Darly fell. He got up again and followed us to the tree.
But then he shouted, "I've dropped my camera!" He went back to look for it but he didn't return.
(5) We searched for an hour but we couldn't find him.
That was the last time we ever saw him. **(6) + (7)**

3 Einen englischen Text zusammenfassen

Wenn du eine Geschichte nacherzählst oder Informationen aus einem Text weitergibst, musst du den Inhalt immer kürzen. Dabei darfst du weder etwas Wichtiges vergessen, noch etwas Unwichtiges beibehalten. Diese Tipps können dir helfen, Informationen zu sammeln bzw. eine gute Zusammenfassung zu schreiben.

	Tipps	Fiktional	Nicht fiktional
1	Copy the text so that you can write on it or mark it.	Stelle sicher, dass du genügend Platz am Rand hast und dass der Zeilenabstand groß genug ist, um zwischen die Zeilen zu schreiben.	
2	Decide how you want to mark the text.	Du kannst Textmarker verwenden oder Bemerkungen an den Rand schreiben. Oft hilft es, verschiedene Farben für verschiedene Punkte einzusetzen.	
3	Read the text again.	Markiere wichtige Dinge / Stellen: z.B. Wörter, Sinnabschnitte und Textteile, Charakterzüge, Atmosphäre, spannende Sätze, …	Markiere wichtige Dinge / Stellen: z.B. Zahlen, Haupt- und Nebenthemen, Argumente oder Namen, die dir wichtig erschei-nen, …
4	Ask questions as you read. (Who? Where? What? When? Why? How?)	Wer sind die Charaktere? Wo befinden sie sich? Was machen sie? Was passiert? Wann passiert es? Warum passiert es? Wie endet die Geschichte?	Welche Infos gibt es zu dem Thema? Welche Argumente werden aufgeführt? Was ist die Schlussfolgerung?
5	Write a rough draft.	Benutze deine eigenen Worte. Wähle einfache Vokabeln und Sätze. Sei sachlich. Füge nicht deine eigene Meinung oder die anderer ein.	
6	Mention only what is important.	Zusammenfassungen sind immer kürzer als der Text. Um eine Kürzung zu erreichen, sollst du Unwichtiges weglassen. Nenne z.B. keine Beispiele, Ausschmückungen, Zitate oder direkte Rede. Verwende auch sprachliche Kürzungen, z.B. das Zusammenziehen von Begriffen zu einer Sachgruppe (*milk, butter, bread = food*).	
7	Write a summary or a report.	Verwende das *simple present*.	Verwende die Zeit, in der der Text geschrieben wurde.

4 Texte verfassen

Anbei findest du acht Schritte *(steps)*, die dir helfen können einen guten Text zu schreiben.

1	Task	Was genau ist deine Aufgabe? Was für einen Text sollst du schreiben? Wozu? Worüber?
2	Content	Welche Punkte musst du erwähnen?
3	Type of text	Welche Merkmale hat ein solcher Text?
4	Plan	Mache einen Entwurf. Vergewissere dich, dass du keine Punkte vergessen hast.
5	Words and phrases	Welche *key words* gibt es zu dem Thema? Benutze ein Wörterbuch, falls du Hilfe brauchst. Fallen dir sogar schon ganze Sätze ein? Sammle alle Wörter, Halbsätze und Sätze in einer *mind map*.
6	First copy	Schreibe einen ersten Entwurf. Lass zwischen den Zeilen Platz frei, damit du Korrekturen einfügen kannst.
7	Partner check	Bitte einen Partner / eine Partnerin, deinen Text zu lesen. Versteht er / sie ihn? Baue seine / ihre Korrekturen in deinen Text mit ein.
8	Final copy	Schreibe den Text neu.

VORSICHT! Es gibt viele *false friends* und Fallen im Englischen. Das heißt, dass es manche gleich aussehende Wörter im Englischen und Deutschen gibt, die in den beiden Sprachen aber etwas anderes bedeuten. Hier sind ein paar Beispiele:

German	English	German	English
Handy	mobile (phone)	praktisch	handy
Gymnasium	grammar school	Turnhalle	gym(nasium)
Technik	technology	Methode	technique
Chips	crisps	Pommes frites	chips
Mappe	folder	Karte	map

The end of a beautiful friendship?

What's your handy number, Susan?

Handy number? What's that?

Grammar summary | **Skills files** | Vocabulary

5 Eine Postkarte schreiben

Zwischen einer Postkarte aus dem englischsprachigen Ausland und einer Postkarte, wie du sie schreiben würdest, gibt es einige Unterschiede – und nicht nur sprachliche.

1	Greeting	*Hi*, oder *Hello*, mit Namen sind üblich. Du kannst auch *Dear* …, sagen. Vergiss das Komma nach dem Namen nicht.
2	Date and place	Im *British English* schreibt man oft Datum und Ortsnamen oben rechts vom Text.
3	First word	Das erste Wort wird groß geschrieben.
4	About you	Sage, wie es dir geht und was du gerade tust. *(present continuous)*
5	The weather	Ein oder zwei kurze Sätze genügen.
6	A report	Sage, was du an welchem Tag gemacht hast. *(simple past)*
7	Future plans	Sage, was du vorhast *(want to, will, would like to, …)* und wann.
8	Short forms	Es wird oft abgekürzt z. B. (*C U …, Luv*)
9	Closing	Vergiss deinen Namen nicht. (*X* = ein Kuss, *O* = eine Umarmung)
10	The name	Anreden wie *Mr, Ms* oder *Mrs* brauchst du nicht in der Adresse.
11	The address	Schreibe die Adresse genauso auf, wie du sie von deinem Freund / deiner Freundin bekommen hast.
12	Postcode	Vergiss die Postleitzahl nicht. Sie steht **nach** dem Ort.
13	Country	Wenn du aus dem Ausland schreibst, gib das Zielland an.

6th August, Dublin **(2)**

Hi, Henry, **(1)**

(3) Just to say we are all well and we're having **(4)** a cool time in Ireland. The weather is great! It has been sunny since we arrived. **(5)** Yesterday we spent **(6)** the day in the zoo. Tomorrow **(7)** we want to go to the coast. We hope we can swim there. Hope **(8)** all is well with you and the family. See you **(8)** when we get back to Glasgow.

(8) Luv Fiona. XOX **(9)**

Henry McFarlane **(10)**

209 Westwind Street **(11)**

Glasgow

GL7 6YT **(12)**

Scotland **(13)**

6 Eine Bewerbung schreiben

Wenn du dich auf Englisch um eine Stelle bewirbst, solltest du neben einem Begleitbrief einen Lebenslauf (*CV*) und Kopien sämtlicher Zeugnisse mitschicken. Im Begleitbrief zeigst du, wie gut du schreiben und berichten kannst. Manchmal wird in der Anzeige ein handschriftlich geschriebener Brief verlangt. Übe, bevor du den Brief endgültig abschickst. Den Musterbrief unten kannst du als Vorlage verwenden.

Suzie Tan **(1)**
239 Gordon Ave. **(2)**
Liverpool LI 56 7TU **(3)**

Mr Richard Rich
Sunshine Film Studios
440 Brighton Road
London SW 6 9OP **(3)**

23 July 2012
Ref: Hol2397 **(5)**

Dear Mr Rich **(4)**

(6) With reference to your ad on the Internet on 20th July, I would like to apply for a job as a studio assistant at Sunshine Film Studios in London.
I finished school on June 26. At the moment I am working as an assistant for a photographer. It is a temporary position and I am looking for a permanent job. I would really like to work in London.
I looked at your company's homepage and some of your projects look very interesting. I have some experience of the film world. I had a holiday job in a TV studio last year. My special skills are organizing and working with people.
As you will see from my CV, I was born in China but I speak and write good English and German. I have some knowledge of Chinese, too. This could be useful with visitors who do not speak English.
I look forward to hearing from you soon.

Yours sincerely **(7)**
Suzie Tan

Encl. **(8)**

1	Name	In englischsprachigen Ländern schreibt man auch zuerst den Vornamen und dann den Nachnamen.
2	Address	Bei Adressen steht die Hausnummer vor dem Straßennamen. Abkürzungen wie *St.* (*Street*), *Ave.* (*Avenue*), *Cl.* (*Close*), *Pde.* (*Parade*) sind üblich.
3	Postal codes	… sind unterschiedlich in verschiedenen Ländern. Falls du an eine Firma schreibst, schreibe die Adresse genau so, wie sie in der Anzeige steht.
4	Dear …,	Schreibe *Sir or Madam*, wenn du den Namen der Person nicht kennst. Bei Männernamen schreibe *Mr*, bei Frauennamen *Ms*.
5	Ref:	… bedeutet *reference* oder Betreff.
6	The first word	… schreibt man immer groß.
7	Closing	Wenn du die Anrede *Sir or Madam* verwendest, dann schreibst du *Yours faithfully*. Ansonsten *Yours sincerely*. Vergiss das ‚s' bei *Yours* nicht.
8	Encl.	= *enclosed* verwendest du, wenn du weitere Unterlagen beilegst (= Anlagen).

7 Einen Lebenslauf (CV) auf Englisch schreiben

Auf S. 74 siehst du einen teilweise ausgefüllten, englischen Lebenslauf (*CV*). **VORSICHT!** Es ist im englischsprachigen Raum nicht üblich, ein Foto mitzuschicken. Hier sind die wichtigsten Angaben:

1	Name	Vorname, dann Nachname
2	Address	mit Postleitzahl und Land
3	Tel.	mit internationaler Vorwahl
4	Email	Prüfe, ob du sie richtig geschrieben hast!
5	Date of birth	*British English* = Tag / Monat / Jahr *American English* = Monat / Tag / Jahr
6	Place of birth	Stadt + Land
7	Primary school	Voller Name und Adresse + Angabe der Jahreszahlen von … bis …
8	Secondary school	Voller Name und Adresse + Angabe der Jahreszahlen von … bis …
9	Examinations	Name und Datum der Prüfungen
10	Skills	Fähigkeiten und Fertigkeiten, die für den Job wichtig sind z. B.: *computer, photography*
11	Work experience	Praktika und Jobs, die du gemacht hast: Wo? Was? Wann?
12	Interests	Hobbys, Sport, ehrenamtliche Tätigkeiten usw.
13	Referees	Lehrer, Trainer, Arbeitgeber, … (Name, Adresse, Telefonnummer)

CV
CV (curriculum vitae) ist ein lateinischer Begriff und heißt übersetzt „course of life" (= Lebenslauf).

Referees
Falls der Arbeitgeber sich für dich interessiert, wird er sich mit deinen *referees* in Verbindung setzen. Du benötigst für deinen Arbeitgeber möglicherweise 2–3 Empfehlungsschreiben von *referees*. Sie sollten den Arbeitgeber über deine Persönlichkeit und deine Leistungen im Job informieren. (Bei Bewerbungen im englischsprachigen Raum bekommst du deine Empfehlungsbriefe nicht zu sehen.)

8 Eine formelle E-Mail schreiben

Wie bei einem formellen Brief, schreibst du in einer formellen E-Mail eine Anrede, eine Einleitung und ein paar abschließende Worte.

Der Betreff (*Re*) sagt, worum es geht.	*Re:*
Wenn du den Namen der angesprochenen Person nicht kennst, verwende die Form in Klammern.	*Dear (Sir or Madam) Mr / Ms … ,*
Das erste Wort wird groß geschrieben.	*With reference to your …*
Sei immer höflich, auch wenn du dich beschweren willst.	*Would it be possible to … ?* *I'd be very grateful if you could …* *I look forward to hearing from you.*
Verwende die richtige Schlussformel.	*Yours faithfully / sincerely* *…*

9 Sich auf ein Vorstellungsgespräch vorbereiten

Es ist sehr wichtig, sich auf das Gespräch gut vorzubereiten. Dann kannst du dich während des Vorstellungsgesprächs besser auf das Wesentliche konzentrieren.

Before the interview	1. Informiere dich über die Stelle / das Land / die Firma / … 2. Überlege dir 2–3 Fragen, die du stellen kannst. 3. Mach dir Gedanken, was du zu dem Vorstellungsgespräch anziehst: einen Anzug / Rock / eine Jeans? Deine Kleidung muss auf jeden Fall sauber und gepflegt sein. Trage nicht zu viel Schmuck / Make-up. 4. Bereite dich darauf vor, Fragen des Interviewers zu beantworten.
During the interview	1. Versuche dich zu entspannen. Schau den Interviewer an und lächle! Gib ihm / ihr die Hand, wenn er / sie es möchte. Deine ersten Worte sind wichtig. 2. Achte darauf, wie der Interviewer mit dir redet: Formell? Freundlich? 3. Mach dir keine Sorgen, wenn du nicht alles verstehst. Der Interviewer weiß, dass dein Englisch nicht perfekt ist. Sei ehrlich!

You can ask on the phone	What do I need to bring with me? (Do you pay travel costs?)	
The interviewer could say	Formal: Good morning / afternoon / …, Mr / Ms … Nice to meet you. Please take a seat / sit down, Mr / Ms …	Informal: Hi / Hello, Pete / Sue / … ! Take a seat!
The interviewer could ask	Why are you interested in this job? Have you worked abroad before? What are your best subjects? What would you do if you had a difficult customer? / … Do you have any questions?	
If you don't understand something, you can ask	Could you repeat the question, please? Excuse me. Could you say that again, please? Excuse me. What does (the word) … mean? I'm sorry. Could you speak more slowly, please?	
You can ask at the interview	How big is your company? How many people work here?	

| Grammar summary | **Skills files** | Vocabulary

10 Hörtexte verstehen

Vor dem Hören:
Es hilft dir, folgende Punkte zu klären, bevor du versuchst, einen Hörtext zu verstehen:

1. Kontext: Wo kommt der Text her? Was weißt du schon über solche Texte?

Medien			Öffentliche Ansagen			Persönliche Gespräche im Alltag		
Radio	TV	…	Bahnhof	Flughafen	…	live	Telefon	…
Hörspiel, Interview, Film			Z. B. Ansage			Anruf, Gespräch, …		
Oft handelt es sich um einen Bericht oder ein Interview.			Die gesuchte Info kann mit einem Schlüsselwort herausgehört werden. Der Rest ist unwichtig.			Du kannst immer nachfragen, wenn du etwas nicht verstanden hast.		

2. Vorwissen: Was kann dir sonst noch beim Erschließen helfen?

Der Titel	Ein Bild	Die Einführung	Sonstige Kenntnisse
… kann bei einem Film oder einer Sendung hilfreich sein.	… hilft oft dabei, sich ein Bild vom Sprecher bzw. von einer anderen Person / Personen zu machen.	… gibt Hintergrundinformationen bzw. erklärt die Situation.	Wie ist die Person, mit der du redest? Wie könnte sie reagieren?

3. Was möchtest du von dem Text erfahren? (Wer? Wann? Was? Wie? Wo? Warum?)

Allgemeines	Bestimmte Details	Eine Information
Was ist das Hauptthema? Um welches Problem / welchen Inhalt geht es?	Wer redet? Welche Angaben werden zu einem Problem / Thema gemacht?	Detaillierte Angaben zu einer bestimmten Frage, z. B. „Wann fährt der nächste Zug?"

Während des Hörens:
Mach dir Notizen.
1. Falls du dir mehrere Punkte notieren willst, kannst du eine Liste, eine *mind map* oder eine Tabelle anfertigen.
2. Hör dir den Text bei einer Prüfung zwei- oder dreimal an. Im Alltag ist das nicht möglich, aber dann kannst du immer jemanden fragen.
3. Prüfe, ob du alle Infos hast, die du brauchst.

Nach dem Hören:
Erledige sämtliche Aufgaben mithilfe deiner Notizen. Falls du mit einem Partner / einer Partnerin zusammenarbeitest, vergleicht eure Ergebnisse.

11 Ein Interview mit jemandem führen

Bevor du ein Interview führst, ist es wichtig, dass du versuchst im Voraus etwas über die Person bzw. das Thema zu erfahren. So kannst du leichter Fragen stellen. Das Interview wird dadurch interessanter.

Tipps	Im Studio	Auf der Straße
1. Be polite.	Good morning / afternoon … My name is / I'm … Thank you for coming to the studio / …	Excuse me. I'm from … School. May I ask you a question about / your opinion on …?
2. Prepare your questions.		
Beginne mit einem Fragewort.	**Who** do you …? / **What** have you …? / **Why** did you …?	**What** is your opinion on …?
Beginne mit einem Verb.	**Can** you tell me …? / **Have** you ever …? / **Is** it true that …?	**Do** you think people should …? **Can** you remember …?
Beginne mit einer höflichen Einladung / Aufforderung.	**Please, tell** us about … / **explain** …	**Could you** say something about …? **Would you** be prepared to give us your opinion on …?
3. Say goodbye.		
Bedanke dich und sage noch etwas Nettes.	**Thank you** very much … That was very interesting / … **We hope** you enjoy your stay in …	**Thank you** Sir / Madam / … You have been very helpful. **Have a nice day.**

12 Eine Präsentation vorbereiten

1. Schreibt zunächst ein Handout und macht Kopien für die Klasse. Hier ein Beispiel:

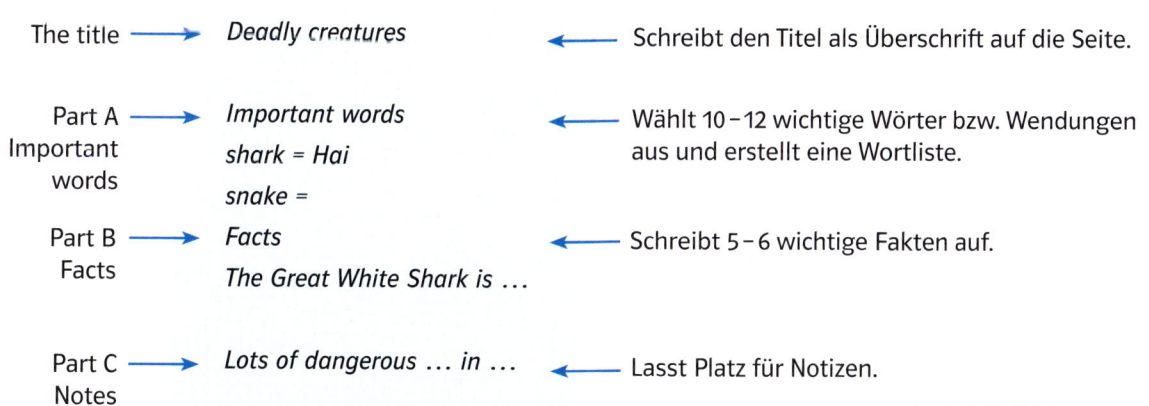

The title	*Deadly creatures*	← Schreibt den Titel als Überschrift auf die Seite.
Part A Important words	*Important words* *shark = Hai* *snake =*	← Wählt 10–12 wichtige Wörter bzw. Wendungen aus und erstellt eine Wortliste.
Part B Facts	*Facts* *The Great White Shark is …*	← Schreibt 5–6 wichtige Fakten auf.
Part C Notes	*Lots of dangerous … in …*	← Lasst Platz für Notizen.

2. Wählt eine Präsentationsform, die ihr interessant findet und bei der ihr eure Talente am besten anwenden könnt. Hier ein paar Beispiele:

A display
(talents: drawing, designing)

A demonstration (talents: making / explaining things)

A sales talk
(talents: public speaking)

A discussion
(talents: speaking, working in a group)

A performance
(talents: singing, performing, acting)

A computer presentation
(talents: using equipment, typing)

Weitere Präsentationsformen, die ihr in diesem Buch findet, sind:
a web page, an advert, an interview, a talk show, a PowerPoint presentation, a reading, a quiz, a summary, a report, a talk, a gallery walk.

3. Tipps für eine PowerPoint-Präsentation:

Tipps
1. Plan your presentation on paper first.
2. Write down a title.
3. Write down the aspects of the topic as a list.
4. Write a few key words on each aspect.
5. Start your PowerPoint programme.
6. Type the title on to one 'page' and your key words on to the other 'pages'. Use your key words in sentences during your presentation.
7. Use pictures and diagrams to improve your presentation.

4. Überprüft, ob eure Mitschüler/innen alles verstanden haben, was ihr ihnen gezeigt bzw. erzählt habt.

A written test	Das können z. B. Fragen, ein Lückentext, ein beschriftetes Diagramm, ein Quiz, ein Kreuzworträtsel, ein Fehlertext bzw. ein Fehlerbild sein.
An oral test	Spiele aller Art: Rollenspiele, Ratespiele, Nacherzählungen, Interviews, Zusammenfassungen, … , z. B.: Ein Kartenspiel: Schreibe Fragen auf Kärtchen. Die anderen ziehen eine Karte und beantworten die Frage.

13 Eine Diskussion / Debatte durchführen

Es gibt viele verschiedene Arten einer Diskussion / Debatte. Folgende Tipps und Redewendungen können euch helfen:

	Tipps	Ausdrücke
1	Einigt euch auf eine Aussage (*statement / motion*).	*I think … is a good statement.* *I'd like to suggest … as our statement.* *Let's vote on it. Who's for / against the statement …*
2	Schreibt sie an die Tafel.	*Statement: Everybody should work for a short time in another country.*
3	Wer macht den Vorsitz? Er / Sie muss die Diskussion / Debatte mithilfe der Sätze rechts leiten.	*Good morning / afternoon.* *Our statement for today's discussion is: …* *Speakers for / against the statement are …* *The first speaker for / against the statement is …* *… , it's your turn. You may speak now.* *Thank you … . Your time is up.*
4	Die Sprecher sammeln Argumente für und gegen die Aussage.	*I agree / don't agree with the statement.* *In my opinion …* *I think it is wrong / important to say that …*
5	Der / Die Vorsitzende fragt, ob andere ihre Meinung äußern möchten.	*Yes, … , what would you like to say?*
6	Der / Die Vorsitzende beendet die Diskussion / Debatte und fordert zur Abstimmung auf.	*Please raise your hand if you are for / against the statement.* *The results of the vote are … for and … against the statement.*

14 Think-Pair-Share (T-P-S)

Du liest und hörst in der Klasse oft: *Compare your answers with a partner, then report to the class.* Dies wird *Think-Pair-Share* genannt. So funktioniert es:
- Mach dir Gedanken zu der Aufgabe und notiere sie. Dein Lehrer kann dir eine zeitliche Grenze von z. B. 5 Minuten geben.
- Finde eine/n Partner/in. Lest euch eure Notizen gegenseitig vor. Zeig sie deinem/r Partner/in nicht! Dies ist eine Sprechaktivität.
- Korrigiert eure Notizen, wenn ihr einen Fehler findet oder fügt neue Informationen hinzu, wenn eine/r von euch eine bessere Idee hat.
- Du oder dein/e Partner/in präsentiert eure gemeinsamen Ideen der Klasse, oder wenn die Aufgabe lang genug ist, stellt ihr sie beide abwechselnd vor.

15 Cheat sheet

Cheat sheet heißt auf Deutsch *Spickzettel* und ist eine gute Möglichkeit, einen Text zusammenzufassen und eine kurze Präsentation darüber zu halten. So funktioniert es:
- Geh den Text durch und notiere Schlüsselbegriffe und wichtige Ausdrücke auf ein kleines Stück Papier. Diese Schlüsselbegriffe enthalten die wichtigsten Informationen des Textes.
- Gehe deine Notizen durch und streiche alle Wörter durch, die nicht absolut notwendig sind! Idealerweise solltest du nur einen Schlüsselbegriff für jeden Teil des Textes haben.
- Verwende deine Liste *(cheat sheet)*, um deine Präsentation zu halten. Die Schlüsselbegriffe helfen dir, dir zu merken, was du sagen willst, aber du solltest soweit wie möglich deine eigenen Worte benutzen. Wiederhole nicht einfach den Originaltext!

16 Gallery walk

Am Ende vieler Gruppenarbeiten in der Klasse werdet ihr einen Text, z. B. eine E-Mail oder vielleicht ein Poster produziert haben. Ein *gallery walk* ist eine Möglichkeit, eure Arbeitsergebnisse in der Klasse zu zeigen. So funktioniert es:
- Hängt die Ergebnisse aller Gruppen im Klassenraum auf und verteilt sie soweit voneinander entfernt wie möglich.
- Dann schaut ihr euch jede Gruppenarbeit im Klassenzimmer an.
- Wenn du bei deiner Arbeit angekommen bist, halte dort an und sei bereit, sie zu erklären und Fragen der Klasse hierzu zu beantworten. Jede/r in deiner Gruppe sollte hierzu in der Lage sein.
- Fahrt in dieser Weise fort, bis jede/r alle Arbeiten gesehen hat.
- Zum Schluss diskutiert ihr die Ergebnisse in der Klasse. Welches war das beliebteste / interessanteste / am besten präsentierte? Warum?

Grundwortschatz und Zahlen

Wochentage, Monatsnamen, Subjektpronomen (*he, she, it* usw.) und Wörter, die im Deutschen und Englischen ähnlich oder identisch sind (z. B. *jeans*), werden als bekannt vorausgesetzt und sind im Folgenden nicht aufgeführt.

A
a/an ein(e)
about über; ungefähr
activity Aktivität
address Adresse
after nach
afternoon Nachmittag
again wieder
against gegen
age Alter
airport Flughafen
all alle(s)
already schon, bereits
also auch
always immer
a.m. vormittags *(nur nach Uhrzeiten)*
America Amerika
American amerikanisch; Amerikaner/in
and und
animal Tier
another noch eine(r, s), ein(e) andere(r, s)
answer; to answer Antwort; beantworten
any irgendein(e)
apple Apfel
to arrive ankommen
as als
to ask (questions) fragen, (Fragen) stellen
at an, auf, in, bei
at home zu Hause
autumn Herbst
away weg

B
back zurück
bad schlecht, schlimm
bathroom Badezimmer
to be (was/were, been) sein
beach Strand
beautiful schön
because weil
bed Bett
bedroom Schlafzimmer
to begin (began, begun) anfangen
below unter, unten
best beste(r, s)
better besser
big groß
bike/bicycle Fahrrad
bird Vogel
birthday Geburtstag
bit (a bit) (ein) bisschen
black schwarz
blue blau
book Buch
boring langweilig
bottle Flasche
box Schachtel, Kiste, Kasten, Kästchen
boy Junge
boyfriend Freund
bread Brot
breakfast Frühstück
Britain Großbritannien
British britisch
brother Bruder
bus Bus
but aber
to bring (brought, brought) bringen
to buy (bought, bought) kaufen
by von; mit

C
cake Kuchen
called namens
can können
car Auto
cat Katze
centre Zentrum
chair Stuhl
child, children Kind(er)
cinema Kino
city (Groß)stadt
class (Schul)klasse, Kurs
clock (Wand)uhr
coffee Kaffee
coke Cola
cold kalt
colour Farbe
to come (came, come) kommen
to cook kochen
to copy kopieren, abschreiben
correct; to correct korrekt, richtig; korrigieren
to cost (cost, cost) kosten
to count zählen
country, countries Land, Länder
to cover decken, bedecken, abdecken
cupboard Schrank

D
dad Papa
to dance tanzen
dancer Tänzer/in
date Datum
daughter Tochter
day Tag
desk Schreibtisch
dialogue Dialog
dictionary Wörterbuch
different verschieden, unterschiedlich
difficult schwierig, schwer
dinner Abendessen
to do (did, done) machen, tun
dog Hund
door Tür
drink; to drink (drank, drunk) Getränk, Trinken; trinken

E
ear Ohr
early früh
east Ost
easy leicht
to eat (ate, eaten) essen
egg Ei
English Englisch; englisch
evening Abend
every jede(r,s)
everywhere überall
example; for example Beispiel; zum Beispiel
Excuse me! Entschuldigung!
exercise Übung
expensive teuer
eye Auge

F
false falsch
family Familie
famous berühmt
far weit, fern
fast schnell
father Vater
favourite lieblings-
to feel (felt, felt) fühlen
to fill in ausfüllen
to find (found, found) finden
to find out herausfinden
fine fein, schön
finish beenden, abschließen, fertigstellen
firm Firma
first erste(r, s)
fish Fisch
flower Blume, Blüte
to fly (flew, flown) fliegen
food Essen, Nahrung
foot, feet Fuß, Füße
football Fußball
for für
to forget (forgot, forgotten) vergessen
form Form; Formular
free frei, kostenlos
free time Freizeit
friend Freund
friendly freundlich
from von
fruit Obst
full voll, vollständig
fun Spaß

G
game Spiel
garden Garten
German Deutsch; deutsch
Germany Deutschland
to get (got, got) bekommen, erhalten
to get up aufstehen
girl Mädchen
girlfriend Freundin
to give (gave, given) geben
glass Glas
to go (went, gone) gehen
good gut
good morning guten Morgen
goodbye auf Wiedersehen
grass Gras, Rasen
great großartig
green grün
guitar Gitarre

guy Typ, Kerl
guest Gast

H
hair Haar
half halb
hand Hand
to happen geschehen, passieren
happy glücklich
hard hart, schwierig
hat Hut
to hate hassen, gar nicht mögen
to have (had, had) haben
head Kopf
to hear (heard, heard) hören
hello hallo
help; to help Hilfe; helfen
her ihr(e)
here hier
hi hallo
high hoch
him ihm, ihn
his sein(e)
holiday Urlaub, Ferien
home Zuhause
homework Hausaufgabe
hot heiß, scharf
hour Stunde
house Haus
how many wie viele
how old wie alt
hungry hungrig
husband Ehemann

I
idea Idee, Vorstellung
if wenn, falls, ob
important wichtig
in; into in; in … hinein
in front of vor
interested (in) interessiert (an)
interesting interessant
its sein(e), ihr(e)

J
job Arbeit, Beruf
just einfach, nur, gerade

K
kid Kind
kilometre Kilometer
to know (knew, known) wissen, kennen

L
language Sprache
large weit, groß
last letzte(r, s)
late (zu) spät
to learn lernen, erfahren
left links
lesson Unterrichtsstunde
Let's … Lass/lasst uns …
letter Brief
light Licht; leicht
like wie
to like mögen
life, lives Leben
to listen (zu)hören
little klein, wenig
to live leben, wohnen
living room Wohnzimmer
long lang
to look at betrachten, ansehen
lots of, a lot of viel(e)
loud laut
to love lieben, sehr gern mögen
lunch Mittagessen

M
magazine Zeitschrift
to make (made, made) machen
man, men Mann, Männer
many viele
map (Land)karte
me mir, mich
to mean (meant, meant) bedeuten
meal Mahlzeit
to meet (met, met) treffen, kennen lernen
metre Meter
midday Mittag
middle Mitte; mittlere(r, s)
midnight Mitternacht
mile Meile
milk Milch
minute Minute
mistake Fehler
(at the) moment (im) Moment
money Geld
month Monat
more mehr
morning Morgen
most die meisten
mother Mutter
motor bike Motorrad
movie (US) Kinofilm
Mr Herr (Anrede)
Mrs Frau (Anrede für verheiratete Frau)
Ms Frau (Anrede)
mum Mama
music Musik
must müssen
my mein(e)

N
name Name
near nahe
never nie(mals)
new neu
next nächste(r, s)
nice nett, schön, hübsch
night Nacht
no nein; kein/e
noise Lärm, Geräusch
north Nord
not nicht
nothing nichts
now jetzt
number Zahl, Nummer

O
o'clock Uhr
of von, aus
of course natürlich
office Büro
often oft, häufig
old alt
on an, auf, bei, in
one day eines Tages
only nur, erst
open; to open offen, geöffnet; öffnen
or oder
other andere(r,s)
our unser(e)

P
p.m. nachmittags (nur nach Uhrzeiten)
page Seite
paper Papier
parents Eltern
part Teil
partner Partner(in)
to pay (paid, paid) (be)zahlen
pen Stift, Füller
people Leute, Volk
perhaps vielleicht
person Person
phone Telefon
photo(graph) Foto(graf)
picture Bild
place Platz, Ort, Stelle
plane Flugzeug
to play spielen
please bitte
police Polizei
potato Kartoffel
pound Pfund
price Preis
to put (put, put) setzen, legen, stellen

Q
quarter Viertel
question Frage
quick(ly) schnell
quiz Ratespiel

R
rain; to rain Regen; regnen
to read (read, read); read out lesen; vorlesen
really wirklich
red rot
remember sich erinnern, daran denken
rich reich
to ride (rode, ridden) reiten; fahren (mit dem Auto, Fahrrad)
right richtig; rechts
right now gerade jetzt
river Fluss
road Straße
room Zimmer, Raum
to run (ran, run) laufen, rennen

S
sad traurig
same der-/die-/dasselbe
to say (said, said) sagen
school Schule
Scotland Schottland
secretary Sekretärin
sea Meer
second zweite(r, s)
to see (saw, seen) sehen, verstehen
to sell verkaufen
to send (sent, sent) schicken, senden
sentence Satz
sheep Schaf
shoe Schuh
shop Geschäft, Laden
shopping Einkaufen
short kurz
to shut (shut, shut) schließen
to sing (sang, sung) singen
sister Schwester
to sit (sat, sat) sitzen
to sleep (slept, slept) schlafen
slow langsam
small klein
snow Schnee
so so
some einige

something etwas
sometimes manchmal
son Sohn
song Lied
soon bald
(I'm) sorry. Tut mir Leid.
south Süden
to speak (spoke, spoken) sprechen
spring Frühling
to stand (stood, stood) stehen
to start anfangen, beginnen
story Geschichte
street Straße
strong stark, kräftig
student Schüler(in), Student(in)
suddenly plötzlich
sugar Zucker
summer Sommer
sun Sonne
sure sicher
to swim (swam, swum) schwimmen

T

table Tabelle, Tisch
to take (took, taken) nehmen, brauchen, dauern
to talk reden, sprechen
tall groß
tea Tee
teacher Lehrer(in)
television Fernsehen
to tell (told, told) erzählen, sagen
thanks; thank you danke
that der/die/das
their ihr(e)
them sie, ihnen
then dann
there dort
there is/are es gibt
these diese
thing Ding, Sache
to think (thought, thought) denken, glauben, meinen
third dritte
this diese(r, s)
those diese
time Zeit
times Mal
tired müde
to an, auf, nach, zu
today heute
tomorrow morgen
too auch; zu
town Stadt
train Zug
to travel reisen, fahren
tree Baum
trousers Hose
true wahr, echt
to try versuchen

U

under unter
to understand (understood, understood) verstehen
to use benutzen, verwenden
usually gewöhnlich

V

very sehr
to visit besuchen

W

to wait warten
to wake up (woke, woken) aufwachen, aufwecken
to walk gehen, laufen, spazieren
wall Wand
to want wollen
to wash waschen
to watch beobachten, zuschauen
water Wasser
to wear (wore, worn) tragen
weather Wetter
week Woche
weekend Wochenende
welcome willkommen
well gut; gesund; also
west Westen
what was
what time um wie viel Uhr
when wann

where wo
which welche(r, s)
white weiß
who wer, wem, wen
why warum
wife, wives Ehefrau, Ehefrauen
to win (won, won) gewinnen
window Fenster
winter Winter
with mit, bei
without ohne
woman, women Frau, Frauen
wonderful herrlich, traumhaft, wundervoll
word Wort
work; to work Arbeit; arbeiten
world Welt
to write (wrote, written) schreiben
wrong falsch

Y

year Jahr
years old Jahre alt
yellow gelb
yes ja
yesterday gestern
young jung
your dein(e), euer/eure

Zahlen

Cardinal numbers			
1	one	17	seventeen
2	two	18	eighteen
3	three	19	nineteen
4	four	20	twenty
5	five	21	twenty-one
6	six	22	twenty-two
7	seven	30	thirty
8	eight	31	thirty-one
9	nine	40	forty
10	ten	50	fifty
11	eleven	60	sixty
12	twelve	70	seventy
13	thirteen	80	eighty
14	fourteen	90	ninety
15	fifteen	100	a hundred
16	sixteen	110	a hundred and ten

Ordinal numbers			
1st	first	17th	seventeenth
2nd	second	18th	eighteenth
3rd	third	19th	nineteenth
4th	fourth	20th	twentieth
5th	fifth	21st	twenty-first
6th	sixth	22nd	twenty-second
7th	seventh	30th	thirtieth
8th	eighth	31st	thirty-first
9th	ninth	40th	fortieth
10th	tenth	50th	fiftieth
11th	eleventh	60th	sixtieth
12th	twelfth	70th	seventieth
13th	thirteenth	80th	eightieth
14th	fourteenth	90th	ninetieth
15th	fifteenth	100th	hundredth
16th	sixteenth		

1,000 a thousand · **1,000,000 (1m)** a million · **1,000,000,000 (1bn)** a billion
1.5 one point five • **2.73** two point seven three · **27%** twenty-seven per cent
½ a half · **¼** a quarter · **¾** three quarters · **⅓** a third · **⅕** a fifth
£1.50 one pound fifty · **99p** ninety-nine p/pence · **$12.20** twelve dollars twenty

| Grammar summary | Skills files | **Vocabulary**

Unitbegleitendes Vokabular

🌐 Videotraining: Englische Aussprache

Perfekte englische Aussprache leicht gemacht: Mit dem Lernprogramm zur englischen Lautschrift können Sie alle Laute einüben. Wählen Sie einfach in der Navigation rechts den entsprechenden Reiter (*Vowels* oder *Consonants*) aus und klicken Sie dann auf das gewünschte phonetische Symbol. Sprechen Sie die Wörter laut nach.

Unter www.klett.de geben Sie bitte den Code unter der Abbildung rechts ein.

🌐 n633sn

Abkürzungen und Zeichen

etw	= etwa	L	= links	1A	Vor den Vokabeln findest du immer die jeweiligen Übungsnummern der Unit.
pl	= Plural, Mehrzahl	R	= rechts		
sb	= somebody				
sth	= something	=	entspricht		
BE	= britisches Englisch	↔	ist das Gegenteil von	**blue**	Vokabel aus Hörtext
AE	= amerikanisches Englisch	→	verwandt mit		
AustrE	= australisches Englisch	!	Achtung		
NewZE	= neuseeländisches Englisch				

Entry English, English everywhere

	entry [ˈentri]	Zugang	
1A	Cologne [kəˈləʊn]	Köln	
	Europe [ˈjʊərəp]	Europa	
	USA [ˌjuːesˈeɪ]	Vereinigte Staaten von Amerika	the United States of America
1B	What about you? [ˌwɒt əbaʊt ˈjuː]	Und du?	
	London [ˈlʌndən]	*Hauptstadt Englands*	
	England [ˈɪŋglənd]	England	
1C	to take it in turns [ˌteɪk ɪt ɪn ˈtɜːnz]	sich abwechseln	There's only one bathroom. We must take it in turns.
2A	native speaker [ˌneɪtɪv ˈspiːkə]	Muttersprachler / in	
	Canada [ˈkænədə]	Kanada	
	worker [ˈwɜːkə]	Arbeiter / in	
	construction worker [kənˈstrʌkʃn wɜːkə]	Bauarbeiter / in	
	G'day [gˈdeɪ]	*(AustrE:)* Guten Tag!	
	nurse [nɜːs]	Krankenschwester, Krankenpfleger	Nurses work in hospitals.
	Australia [ɒsˈtreɪliə]	Australien	
	technician [tekˈnɪʃn]	Techniker / in	*-ician* für Berufe *(electrician, musician)*
	New Zealand [ˌnjuː ˈziːlənd]	Neuseeland	
2C	twins [twɪnz]	Zwillinge	
	painter [ˈpeɪntə]	Maler / in, Anstreicher / in	painter → paint

	decorator ['dekəreɪtə]	Maler/in, Tapezierer/in	
	doctor ['dɒktə]	Arzt, Ärztin	You go to the doctor when you are ill.
	receptionist [rɪ'sepʃənɪst]	Empfangsdame, -mitarbeiter	receptionist → reception
	doctor's receptionist ['dɒktəz rɪ'sepʃənɪst]	Sprechstundenhilfe	
2E	to be called [bi 'kɔːld]	heißen	
3A	Montana [mɒn'tænə]	US-Bundesstaat	
	walking ['wɔːkɪŋ]	Wandern, Spazierengehen	walking ↔ running
	cycling ['saɪklɪŋ]	Fahrradfahren	I love walking and cycling.
	canoeing [kə'nuːɪŋ]	Kanufahren	
	to go on holiday (to) [ˌɡəʊ ɒn 'hɒlɪdeɪ]	Urlaub machen (in)	They go on holiday to Italy every year.
3B	hostel ['hɒstl]	Herberge	
	brochure ['brəʊʃə]	Prospekt, Broschüre	! Betonung
	on the phone [ˌɒn ðə 'fəʊn]	am Telefon	
	hostel warden ['hɒstl wɔːdn]	Herbergsvater/-mutter	
	to complete [kəm'pliːt]	vervollständigen	Complete the sentences with a partner.
	to check [tʃek]	überprüfen, kontrollieren	Can you check the time? Isn't it late?
	mountain ['maʊntɪn]	Berg	
	speaking ['spiːkɪŋ]	am Apparat	
	facilities [fə'sɪlətɪz]	Einrichtung(en), Räumlichkeiten, Ausstattung	The hotel has fantastic facilities.
	dining room ['daɪnɪŋ rʊm]	Esszimmer, Speisesaal	
	washing machine ['wɒʃɪŋ məʃiːn]	Waschmaschine	There's a washing machine for dirty T-shirts.
	much [mʌtʃ]	viel	
	thanks very much [ˌθæŋks veri 'mʌtʃ]	vielen Dank	Thanks very much for your help.
	You're welcome. [jɔː 'welkəm]	Bitte. Gern geschehen.	
	bye [baɪ]	tschüs	→ bye-bye
	access ['ækses]	Zugang, Zugriff	I have access to his computer.
	etc. [et 'setərə]	usw.	
	to contact ['kɒntækt]	sich in Verbindung setzen mit	If you want to contact her, write an email.
3C	main [meɪn]	Haupt-	
	main street ['meɪn striːt]	Hauptstraße	There are lots of shops in the main street.
	movie theater ['muːvi θɪətə]	(AE:) Kino	
	post office ['pəʊst ɒfɪs]	Postamt	Get me some stamps at the post office.
	pharmacy ['fɑːməsi]	(AE:) Apotheke	(BE:) chemist
	swimming pool ['swɪmɪŋ puːl]	Schwimmbad	
4A	celeb [sɪ'leb]	Promi	
	star [stɑː]	Star	the star of the show
	sportspeople ['spɔːtspiːpl]	Sportler	
	singer ['sɪŋə]	Sänger/in	singer → sing
	musician [mjʊ'zɪʃn]	Musiker/in	musician → music → musical
	celebrity [sɪ'lebrɪti]	Prominente/r	There were many celebrities at the party.
	Munich ['mjuːnɪk]	München	
	footballer ['fʊtbɔːlə]	Fußballspieler/in	
	to note down [ˌnəʊt 'daʊn]	notieren, aufschreiben	Listen and note down your answers.
	France [frɑːns]	Frankreich	
	piano [pɪ'ænəʊ]	Klavier	
	tattoo [tæt'uː]	Tätowierung	
	side [saɪd]	Seite	They drive on the left side of the road in Britain.
	body ['bɒdi]	Körper	
	back ['bæk]	Rücken	She has a tattoo on her back.
	actor ['æktə]	Schauspieler	actor → actress
	California [kælɪ'fɔːniə]	Kalifornien	
	once [wʌns]	einmal	I only did it once.
4C	questionnaire [ˌkwestʃə'neə]	Fragebogen	The questionnaire has 100 questions.
	motor bike ['məʊtə baɪk]	Motorrad	

Grammar summary | Skills files | Vocabulary

scooter [ˈskuːtə]	Motorroller	He rides a scooter to work.
inline skates [ˈɪnlaɪn skeɪts]	Inline-Skates	
laptop [ˈlæptɒp]	Laptop, Notebook	
album [ˈælbəm]	Album, CD	
poster [ˈpəʊstə]	Plakat	
musical instrument [ˌmjuːzɪkl ˈɪnstrəmənt]	Musikinstrument	
4D No way! [ˌnəʊ ˈweɪ]	Nie im Leben! Auf gar keinen Fall!	No way! I won't go to her concert.
terrible [ˈterəbl]	furchtbar, fürchterlich	The music was terrible!
5A social [ˈsəʊʃl]	sozial	
networking [ˈnetwɜːkɪŋ]	Netzwerk(-)	
site [saɪt]	Website	
to match [mætʃ]	zuordnen	Match the numbers and letters.
past [pɑːst]	(Uhrzeit:) nach	! half past twelve = halb eins
to [tə]	(Uhrzeit:) vor	
a quarter to [ə ˈkwɔːtə tə]	(Uhrzeit:) Viertel vor	quarter wird wie four ausgesprochen
5B to point to [pɔɪnt ˈtə]	zeigen auf	Point to the right number.
What time is it? [ˌwɒt ˈtaɪm ɪz ɪt]	Wie spät ist es? Wieviel Uhr ist es?	
5C missing [ˈmɪsɪŋ]	fehlend	There's a letter missing.
fashion [ˈfæʃn]	Mode	
company [ˈkʌmpəni]	Unternehmen, Firma	firm
to jog [dʒɒg]	joggen	
subway [ˈsʌbweɪ]	(AE:) U-Bahn	(BE:) underground
to say hello to sb [ˌseɪ həˌləʊ tə]	jdn begrüßen	Say hello to my mother.
apartment [əˈpɑːtmənt]	(AE:) Wohnung	(BE:) flat
supper [ˈsʌpə]	Abendessen	Supper is at 6 o'clock.
5D tip [tɪp]	Tipp, Hinweis	
trick [trɪk]	Trick, Kniff	
5E vocational college [vəʊˌkeɪʃnl ˈkɒlɪdʒ]	Berufsbildende Schule	
to work out [wɜːk ˈaʊt]	trainieren	
fitness club [ˈfɪtnəs klʌb]	Fitnessklub	
6A waiter [ˈweɪtə]	Kellner	waiter → waitress
bus driver [ˈbʌs draɪvə]	Busfahrer/in	
shoe shop [ˈʃuː ʃɒp]	Schuhgeschäft	
shop assistant [ˈʃɒp əsɪstənt]	Verkäufer/in	A shop assistant sells things in the shop.
mechanic [mɪˈkænɪk]	Mechaniker/in	A mechanic often works with cars.
backpacker [ˈbækpækə]	Rucksacktourist/in	
6B conversation [ˌkɒnvəˈseɪʃn]	Gespräch, Unterhaltung	a conversation with sb about sth
trainers [ˈtreɪnəz]	Turnschuhe	
size [saɪz]	Größe	What size shoes do you take?
Just a minute! [ˌdʒʌst ə ˈmɪnɪt]	Einen Moment!	
should [ʃʊd]	sollte/n	It's cold. You should wear a pullover.
thanks a lot [ˌθæŋks ə ˈlɒt]	vielen Dank	
youth [juːθ]	Jugend	young people
youth hostel [ˈjuːθ hɒstl]	Jugendherberge	A youth hostel is a cheap place to stay.
ticket [ˈtɪkɪt]	Fahrschein	Buy a ticket, then take the bus.
euro [ˈjʊərəʊ]	Euro	! Betonung
to sit down [sɪt ˈdaʊn]	sich (hin)setzen	to sit down ↔ to stand up
to go off [gəʊ ˈɒf]	losgehen	
most of the time [ˈməʊst əv ðə ˌtaɪm]	meistens	usually
maybe [ˈmeɪbi]	vielleicht	perhaps
to stop [stɒp]	anhalten, stehen bleiben, (Motor:) ausgehen	The bus always stops here.
engine [ˈendʒɪn]	Motor	Most cars have the engine in the front.
to start [stɑːt]	starten	to start ↔ to stop
electrical [ɪˈlektrɪkl]	elektrisch	

to test [test]	testen, ausprobieren	electrical → electricity
ready ['redi]	bereit, fertig	If you are ready, let's go.
to order ['ɔːdə]	bestellen	Let's order steaks.
sir [sɜː]	mein Herr	Good morning, sir.
yeah [jeə]	ja	
menu ['menjuː]	Speisekarte	! Nicht verwechseln mit 'Menü'.
steak [steɪk]	Steak	
fries [fraɪz]	(AE:) Pommes	(BE:) chips
vegetables ['vedʒtəblz]	Gemüse	! Betonung
pea [piː]	Erbse	
carrot ['kærət]	Karotte, Möhre	
bean [biːn]	Bohne	
medium rare [ˌmiːdiəm 'reə]	(Steak:) medium	medium rare ↔ well done
certainly ['sɜːtnli]	gewiss, sicherlich	I certainly want to come to your birthday party.
to book [bʊk]	reservieren, buchen	I want to book a holiday in Italy.
single room ['sɪŋgl ˌruːm]	Einzelzimmer	
double room ['dʌbl ˌruːm]	Doppelzimmer	
credit card ['kredɪt ˌkɑːd]	Kreditkarte	
to reserve [rɪ'sɜːv]	reservieren	Can I reserve a table?
to call [kɔːl]	anrufen; nennen, rufen	to phone
to look forward to doing sth [ˌlʊk 'fɔːwəd tə]	sich auf etw freuen	I look forward to hearing from you.

7A
verb [vɜːb]	Verb	
married to ['mærɪd to]	verheiratet mit	He's married to my sister.
capital (city) [ˌkæpɪtl 'sɪti]	Hauptstadt	London is the capital of the United Kingdom.
cook [kʊk]	Koch / Köchin	
crown [kraʊn]	Krone	
at work [ət 'wɜːk]	bei der Arbeit	He's not here. He's at work.
to welcome ['welkəm]	wilkommen heißen, begrüßen	
from around the world [frəm əˌraʊnd ðə 'wɜːld]	aus der ganzen Welt	
twice [twaɪs]	zweimal	Listen. I won't tell you twice.
to surf [sɜːf]	surfen	

7C to imagine [ɪ'mædʒɪn] — sich etw vorstellen — It's difficult to imagine, but it's true.
7D phrase [freɪz] — Wendung, Ausdruck
7F next to ['nekst tə] — neben — Can I sit next to you?
7G to choose (chose, chosen) [tʃuːz, tʃəʊz, tʃəʊzən] — wählen, auswählen, aussuchen — ! Doppel 'o'

to watch TV [ˌwɒtʃ tiː'viː]	fernsehen	to watch TV – to see a film
horse [hɔːs]	Pferd	

Unit 1 At college

unit ['juːnɪt]	Lektion	
college ['kɒlɪdʒ]	Hochschule, Berufsbildende Schule, Universität	After school you can go to college.

1B
to search ['sɜːtʃ]	suchen, durchsuchen	
message ['mesɪdʒ]	Nachricht, Mitteilung	
community [kə'mjuːnəti]	Gemeinde	It's a very friendly community here.
community college [kə'mjuːnəti kɒlɪdʒ]	(USA:) College, das ein Zweijahres-studium anbietet, hauptsächlich für Studenten aus der Gegend	
to get to know [ˌget tə 'nəʊ]	kennen lernen	After a week we got to know each other quite well.
to train [treɪn]	eine Ausbildung machen; trainieren	
particularly [pə'tɪkjələli]	vor allem, insbesondere	This is particularly important.
to leave (left, left) [liːv, left, left]	hinterlassen, dalassen; weggehen, verlassen (Schule) abgehen	

| Grammar summary | Skills files | **Vocabulary** |

to get back to [ˌget ˈbæk tə]	sich melden bei	I'll get back to you in the morning.
to hope [həʊp]	hoffen	
worldwide [wɜːldˈwaɪd]	auf der ganzen Welt, weltweit	The company has offices worldwide.
platform [ˈplætfɔːm]	Plattform	
around the world [əˌraʊnd ðə ˈwɜːld]	auf der ganzen Welt	
to organise [ˈɔːgənaɪz]	organisieren	We must organise a meeting as soon as possible.
project [ˈprɒdʒekt]	Projekt	
international [ˌɪntəˈnæʃnl]	international	
visit [ˈvɪzɪt]	Besuch	visit → to visit → visitor
exchange [ɪksˈtʃeɪndʒ]	Austausch	

2A
course [kɔːs]	Kurs, Lehrgang	
business course [ˈbɪznəs kɔːs]	Betriebswirtschaftslehrgang	
marketing company [ˈmɑːkətɪŋ kʌmpəni]	Vertriebsgesellschaft	
full-time [ˈfʊl taɪm]	Ganztags-, Vollzeit-	full-time ↔ part-time
break [breɪk]	Pause	Let's have a break for lunch.
lunch break [ˈlʌntʃ breɪk]	Mittagspause	
athletics [æθˈletɪks]	Leichtathletik	athletics → athlete
to hang out with (hung, hung) [ˌhæŋ ˈaʊt wɪð, hʌŋ, hʌŋ]	mit jdm abhängen, sich mit jdm rumtreiben	

2D
truck [trʌk]	(AE:) Lkw, Lastwagen	(BE:) lorry
truck driver [ˈtrʌk draɪvə]	(AE:) Lastwagenfahrer/in, Fernfahrer/in	
state [steɪt]	Staat, Bundesstaat; staatlich, Staats-	
to flow [fləʊ]	fließen	

3A
high school [ˈhaɪ skuːl]	Oberschule	a school in the USA for kids from 15 to 18
almost [ˈɔːlməʊst]	fast, beinah	Emma is still 17, but she's almost 18.
one day [wʌn ˈdeɪ]	eines Tages	

3B
to offer [ˈɒfə]	bieten, anbieten	Can I offer you a drink?
to last [lɑːst]	dauern	The hot weather doesn't usually last that long.
over [ˈəʊvə]	über	
everyone [ˈevrɪwʌn]	jeder, alle	everybody
whether [ˈweðə]	ob	! Nicht mit *weather* verwechseln.
hairdresser [ˈheəˌdresə]	Friseur/in	Hairdressers wash and cut people's hair.
credit [ˈkredɪt]	*etwa:* Leistungspunkte	
enough [ɪˈnʌf]	genug, genügend	Die zweite Silbe wird 'aff' gesprochen.
even [ˈiːvn]	sogar, noch	She is tall, but her brother is even taller.
between [bɪˈtwiːn]	zwischen	There's a break between lessons.
to need [niːd]	brauchen, benötigen	Tom needs a lot of sleep.
details [ˈdiːteɪlz]	Einzelheiten, Angaben	
subject [ˈsʌbdʒɪkt]	Fach; Thema	
area [ˈeərɪə]	Gebiet	
art [ɑːt]	Kunst, Grafik	! Nicht mit 'Art' verwechseln.
design [dɪˈzaɪn]	Gestaltung, Design	
automotive mechanics [ɔːtəˌməʊtɪv miːˈkænɪks]	Kraftfahrzeugmechanik	
administration [ədˌmɪnɪˈstreɪʃn]	Verwaltung	administration → administer
business administration [ˈbɪznəs ədmɪnɪstreɪʃn]	Betriebswirtschaftslehre	
information technology [ˌɪnfəˌmeɪʃn tekˈnɒlədʒi]	Informationstechnologie	IT is short for information technology.
construction [kənˈstrʌkʃn]	Baugewerbe, Bauwesen	construction → construct
health [helθ]	Gesundheit, Gesundheitswesen	health → healthy
beauty [ˈbjuːti]	Schönheit, Kosmetik	beauty → beautiful
media [ˈmiːdɪə]	Medien	
retail services [ˈriːteɪl sɜːvɪsɪz]	Einzelhandel	

	social work [ˌsəʊʃl ˈwɜːk]	Sozialarbeit	
	child care [ˈtʃaɪld keə]	Kinderbetreuung	
	electronics [ɪˌlekˈtrɒnɪks]	Elektronik	There are many electronics companies in Asia.
	to email [ˈiːmeɪl]	eine E-Mail schreiben	
	toll free [ˈtəʊl friː]	*(AE:)* gebührenfrei	
4A	simple present [ˌsɪmpl ˈpreznt]	einfaches Präsens	
4B	normally [ˈnɔːmli]	üblicherweise, normalerweise	
4C	uncle [ˈʌŋkl]	Onkel	aunt and uncle
	radio station [ˈreɪdiəʊ steɪʃn]	Radiosender	
	technical [ˈteknɪkl]	technisch	technical → technician
	mall [mɔːl]	Einkaufszentrum	Teenagers love hanging out at malls.
4D	information [ˌɪnfəˈmeɪʃn]	Angaben, Information(en)	a piece of information, some information
	astronaut [ˈæstrənɔːt]	Astronaut/in	
4E	negative [ˈnegətɪv]	verneinend, negativ	
	extremely [ɪkˈstriːmli]	äußerst	The weather in Siberia is extremely cold.
	private [ˈpraɪvət]	privat, Privat-	
	planet [ˈplænɪt]	Planet	
4H	electrician [ɪˌlekˈtrɪʃn]	Elektriker/in	electrician → electrical → electricity
	part-time [ˈpɑːt taɪm]	Halbtags-, Teilzeit-	He has a part-time job in the evening.
	practical [ˈpræktɪkl]	praktisch, sinnvoll, vernünftig	practical ↔ theoretical
4I	bottom [ˈbɒtəm]	Ende, *(Seite:)* Fuß	
	to depend on [dɪˈpend ɒn]	abhängen von, ankommen auf	I don't know if I can go on holiday. It depends on how much money I have.
	It depends. [ˌɪt dɪˈpendz]	Kommt darauf an.	
	strange [streɪndʒ]	seltsam, komisch	That's a strange story!
5A	group [gruːp]	Gruppe	
	to compare [kəmˈpeə]	vergleichen	Compare A with B and C.
	capital letter [ˌkæpɪtl ˈletə]	Großbuchstabe	
	noticeboard [ˈnəʊtɪsbɔːd]	Schwarzes Brett	
5B	since [sɪns]	seit	It's a long time since I saw Emily.
	regularly [ˈregjələ]	regelmäßig	
	topic [ˈtɒpɪk]	Thema	
	classroom [ˈklɑːsrʊm]	Klassenzimmer	
	gallery [ˈgæləri]	Galerie	
	walk [wɔːk]	Spaziergang, Rundgang	
V1	stopover [ˈstɒpəʊvə]	Zwischenaufenthalt, Zwischenstation	The stopover was for two hours.
	competition [ˌkɒmpəˈtɪʃn]	Wettbewerb	competition → compete
	prize [praɪz]	Gewinn, Preis	first prize
	before [bɪˈfɔː]	bevor	
	to report to [rɪˈpɔːt tə]	(jdm) Bericht erstatten; sich melden bei	
	sight [saɪt]	Sehenswürdigkeit	In the old city there are many sites to see.
	on the way [ɒn ðə ˈweɪ]	unterwegs	

Unit 2 People and jobs

1A	career [kəˈrɪə]	Beruf, Laufbahn, Karriere	a career as a (singer)
1B	right now [ˌraɪt ˈnaʊ]	im Augenblick, gerade	at the moment
1C	profile [ˈprəʊfaɪl]	Profil, Beschreibung, Porträt	
	fitness trainer [ˈfɪtnəs treɪnə]	Fitnesstrainer	
	personal [ˈpɜːsnl]	persönlich	
	personal trainer [ˌpɜːsnl ˈtreɪnə]	(persönlicher) Fitnesstrainer	
	exercise machine [ˈeksəsaɪz məʃiːn]	Fitnessgerät	
	diet [ˈdaɪət]	Ernährung; Diät	! Aussprache
	healthy [ˈhelθi]	gesund, gesundheitsfördernd	Fruit and vegetables are healthy.
	lifestyle [ˈlaɪfstaɪl]	Lebensweise	

	inside [ˌɪnˈsaɪd]	drinnen	inside ↔ outside
	sports centre [ˈspɔːts sentə]	Sportzentrum	
	hours [ˈaʊəz]	Arbeitszeiten	She works long hours.
	fit [fɪt]	fit, gesund	
	to keep fit (kept, kept) [ˌkiːp ˈfɪt, kept, kept]	sich fit halten	She likes to keep fit. She goes to the gym regularly.
	outside [ˌaʊtˈsaɪd]	draußen	Stay here. It's cold outside.
	stadium [ˈsteɪdɪəm]	Stadion	
2A	each [iːtʃ]	jede/r/s	T-shirts are €5 each.
	mechanical [mɪˈkænɪkl]	mechanisch	
	plant [plɑːnt]	Pflanze	I prefer plants and animals to mechanical things.
	team [tiːm]	Team, Mannschaft, Gruppe	
	gardener [ˈgɑːdnə]	Gärtner/in	
	to look after [lʊk ˈɑːftə]	sich kümmern um, pflegen	He looks after his old parents.
	to cut (cut, cut) [kʌt, kʌt, kʌt]	schneiden	cutting
	to cut grass [ˌkʌt ˈgrɑːs]	Rasen mähen	
	nature [ˈneɪtʃə]	Natur	She loves nature.
	to repair [rɪˈpeə]	reparieren	
	to service [ˈsɜːvɪs]	*(Gerät:)* warten	You should service your car once a year.
	vehicle [ˈvɪəkl]	Fahrzeug	**!** Aussprache
	workshop [ˈwɜːkʃɒp]	Werkstatt	
	around [əˈraʊnd]	ungefähr, zirka	about
	nursery assistant [ˈnɜːsəri əsɪstənt]	Hilfslehrerin im Kindergarten	
	salon [ˈsælɒn]	(Friseur-, Kosmetik-)Salon	
3A	to interview [ˈɪntəvjuː]	interviewen	to interview → an interview
	order [ˈɔːdə]	Reihenfolge	in the right/wrong order
	real [rɪəl]	wirklich, ziemlich, *hier:* sehr	
	top man [ˌtɒp ˈmæn]	*etwa:* Spitzenmann	
	in fact [ɪn ˈfækt]	eigentlich, um genau zu sein	He's rich, in fact he's a millionaire now.
	postman [ˈpəʊstmən]	Postbote	
	mail [meɪl]	Post	
	to deliver [dɪˈlɪvə]	(aus)liefern, *(Post:)* austragen	You order online and they deliver the next day.
	package [ˈpækɪdʒ]	Paket	A package came for you today.
	folks [fəʊks]	Leute	
	busy [ˈbɪzi]	(viel)beschäftigt	**!** Aussprache
	barman [ˈbɑːmən]	Barkeeper	
	crocodile [ˈkrɒkədaɪl]	Krokodil	
	hunter [ˈhʌntə]	Jäger	
3B	to hunt [hʌnt]	jagen	
	to serve [sɜːv]	*(Kunden:)* bedienen, *(Speisen:)* servieren	They serve steak with chips.
	customer [ˈkʌstəmə]	Kunde/Kundin	The customer is always right!
	hairdressing salon [ˌheədresɪŋ ˈsælɒn]	Friseursalon	
3D	litre [ˈliːtə]	Liter	
	newspaper [ˈnjuːspeɪpə]	Zeitung	Tim reads the newspaper every day.
	Here you go. [ˌhɪə ju ˈgəʊ]	Hier, bitte sehr.	
	See you later. [siː jə ˈleɪtə]	Bis dann!	
	battery [ˈbætəri]	Batterie, Akku	My phone battery is empty.
	to phone [fəʊn]	anrufen, telefonieren	
	Darwin [ˈdɑːwɪn]	*Hauptstadt des Northern Territory*	
	beer [bɪə]	Bier	
	ouch! [aʊtʃ]	au!	
	careful [ˈkeəfl]	vorsichtig	She's a good driver. She's very careful.
	to keep still [ˌkiːp ˈstɪl]	ruhig halten	
	to hold (held, held) [həʊld, held, held]	halten, festhalten	Can you hold this package for a moment?

	Watch out! [ˌwɒtʃ ˈaʊt]	Achtung! Vorsicht!	
3F	northern [ˈnɔːðən]	nördlich, Nord-	northern → north
	southern [ˈsʌðən]	südlich, Süd-	southern → south
	eastern [ˈiːstən]	östlich, Ost-	eastern → east
	western [ˈwestən]	westlich, West-	western → west
	life [laɪf]	Leben	life → lives
	population [ˌpɒpjuˈleɪʃn]	Bevölkerung, Einwohnerzahl	
	sheep [ʃiːp]	Schaf, Schafe	1 sheep – 2 sheep
	fly [flaɪ]	Mücke	
4A	to decide [dɪˈsaɪd]	entscheiden	I can't decide. The red one or the blue one?
	to belong [bɪˈlɒŋ]	gehören	This laptop doesn't belong to me.
4B	ill [ɪl]	krank	
4C	present continuous [ˌpreznt kənˈtɪnjuəs]	Verlaufsform des Präsens	
	nursery (school) [ˈnɜːsəri skuːl]	Kindergarten	
	quiet [ˈkwaɪət]	ruhig, still	quiet ↔ noisy
4E	spelling [ˈspelɪŋ]	Schreibweise, Rechtschreibung	The spelling is wrong. Can you do a spell check?
	to lift [lɪft]	heben, hochheben	
	weight [weɪt]	Gewicht	weight → to weigh
	to drive (drove, driven) [draɪv, drəʊv, ˈdrɪvən]	fahren	
4G	kitchen [ˈkɪtʃɪn]	Küche	
	chef [ʃef]	Koch / Köchin	A chef works in the kitchen, not in an office!
	to show sb round [ˌʃəʊ ˈraʊnd]	jdn herumführen	Let me show you round my house.
	typical [ˈtɪpɪkl]	typisch, normal	
	to prepare [prɪˈpeə]	zubereiten, kochen	At the moment I'm preparing a big meal.
	lamb [læm]	Lamm	
	garlic [ˈgɑːlɪk]	Knoblauch	
	sauce [sɔːs]	Soße	
	colleague [ˈkɒliːg]	Kollege / Kollegin	
	over there [ˌəʊvə ˈðeə]	dort drüben	Can you see the dark clouds over there?
	meat [miːt]	Fleisch	
	to get ready [ˌget ˈredi]	sich vorbereiten, sich fertig machen	We leave soon. I must get ready.
4H	to describe [dɪˈskraɪb]	beschreiben	
	shorts [ˈʃɔːts]	kurze Hosen	The shorts are too long.
	foreground [ˈfɔːgraʊnd]	Vordergrund	foreground ↔ background
	to take off [teɪk ˈɒf]	(Flugzeug:) starten, abheben	to take off ↔ to land
5B	model [ˈmɒdl]	Muster, Vorlage	
	postwoman [ˈpəʊstwʊmən]	Postbotin	
V2	visitor [ˈvɪzɪtə]	Besucher / in	
	to complete [kəmˈpliːt]	ausfüllen	

Unit 3 Free time

	free time [ˈfriː ˌtaɪm]	Freizeit	
	education [ˌedʒʊˈkeɪʃn]	Bildung, Ausbildung	You need a good education for a good job.
	belt [belt]	Gürtel	My trousers don't fit, I need a belt.
1A	FE college [ˌefiː ˌkɒlɪdʒ]	Berufsschule	college of further education
	social networking site [ˌsəʊʃl ˈnetwɜːkɪŋ ˌsaɪt]	soziales Netzwerk	to join a social network
1B	to bake [beɪk]	backen	to bake a cake
	to veg [vedʒ]	herumhängen	to hang around with sb
	place [pleɪs]	Ort, Platz, Stelle	My hometown is a great place to live!
2A	driving test [ˈdraɪvɪŋ ˌtest]	Führerschein	
	Highway Code [ˌhaɪweɪ ˈkəʊd]	Straßenverkehrsordnung	
	accident [ˈæksɪdənt]	Unfall	He had a car accident last week.
	theory [ˈθɪəri]	Theorie	

| Grammar summary | Skills files | **Vocabulary**

	popular [ˈpɒpjələ]	beliebt	popular ↔ unpopular
	lyrics [ˈlɪrɪks]	Liedtext, Songtext	(nur Plural!) Do you know the lyrics of that song?
	cycle ride [ˈsaɪkl ˌraɪd]	Fahrradfahrt	a journey on a bike
	photographer [fəˈtɒɡrəfə]	Fotograf/in	She's a photographer, her photos are great.
	first aid [ˌfɜːst ˈeɪd]	Erste Hilfe	
	medical centre [ˈmedɪkl ˌsentə]	Klinikum	
2B	gym [dʒɪm]	Fitnessklub	fitness club
	jewellery [ˈdʒuːəlri]	Schmuck	earrings, rings etc.
2E	really [ˈrɪəli]	wirklich, ziemlich, hier: sehr	real → really
	brilliant [ˈbrɪliənt]	großartig, hervorragend	= great, super
	to be keen on sth [ˌbi ˈkiːn ɒn]	von etw begeistert / angetan sein	to be very interested in sth
	to text sb [tekst]	eine SMS / Kurznachricht schicken	You can text messages on your smartphone.
2F	likes [laɪks]	Vorlieben	the things that you love
	dislike [dɪˈslaɪks]	Abneigung	the things that you hate
3A	to post [pəʊst]	posten, einen Beitrag schreiben	
	part-time job [ˈpɑːt taɪm ˌdʒɒb]	Teilzeitjob	part-time ↔ full-time
	to earn [ɜːn]	verdienen	She has a good job and earns a lot of money.
	barista [bɑːˈriːstə]	Barista, Kaffeezubereiter/in in Espressobar	The espresso the barista made is great.
	to fit sth around sth [fɪt əˈraʊnd]	um etw herum anordnen	
	the best thing of all [ˈbest ˌθɪŋ]	das Beste von allem	
3B	than [ðæn; ðən]	(nach Komparativ:) als	The weather is better than yesterday.
	adjective [ˈædʒəktɪv]	Adjektiv	
	comparative [kəmˈpærətɪv]	Komparativ	
	superlative [suːˈpɜːlətɪv]	Superlativ	
3C	muffin [ˈmʌfɪn]	Muffin, Törtchen	
	cheesecake [ˈtʃiːzkeɪk]	Käsekuchen	
	cookie [ˈkʊki]	(AE:) Keks, Plätzchen	(BE:) biscuit
	sweet [swiːt]	süß	Sugar is sweet.
4D	clothes [ˈkləʊðz]	Kleidung	His clothes are the latest fashion.
4E	by far [baɪ ˈfɑː]	bei Weitem	
	antivirus [ˌæntɪˈvaɪrəs]	Antivirus-	Your computer needs an antivirus software to be safe.
	match [mætʃ]	Spiel	The football match yesterday was great.
	salad [ˈsæləd]	Salat	A tomato salad for me, please.
	burger [ˈbɜːɡə]	Burger	hamburger, cheeseburger
	Death Valley [ˌdeθ ˈvæli]	Tal des Todes	Death Valley is in the USA.
	temperature [ˈtemprətʃə]	Temperatur	
	record [ˈrekɔːd]	Rekord	! Betonung
4F	Canary Wharf [kəˈneəri ˌwɔːf]	Bürogebäudekomplex (Kanaren-Werft)	
	famous [ˈfeɪməs]	berühmt	Stars are famous people.
	airport [ˈeəpɔːt]	Flughafen	London has got five airports.
	Buckingham Palace [ˌbʌkɪŋəm ˈpælɪs]	Buckingham Palast	
	queen [kwiːn]	Königin	queen ↔ king
	Houses of Parliament [ˌhaʊzɪz əv ˈpɑːləmənt]	Parlamentsgebäude	
	London Eye [ˌlʌndən ˈaɪ]	Riesenrad in London	The highest wheel in Europe.
	wheel [wiːl]	Rad	A car has got four wheels.
	underground [ˈʌndəɡraʊnd]	U-Bahn	The London Underground is called the tube.
	system [ˈsɪstəm]	System	! Betonung
	large [lɑːdʒ]	ausgedehnt, großflächig	= very big
	exciting [ɪkˈsaɪtɪŋ]	aufregend, spannend	exciting ↔ boring
5A	survey [ˈsɜːveɪ]	Umfrage	They had a questionnaire for the survey.
	graph [ɡrɑːf]	Diagramm	= diagram
5B	result [rɪˈzʌlt]	Ergebnis	= answer

V3	**mistake** [mɪˈsteɪk]	Fehler, Irrtum	a wrong answer is a mistake
	Brits [brɪts]	(die) Briten	

Unit 4 Products and services

	product [ˈprɒdʌkt]	Produkt	
	service [ˈsɜːvɪs]	Dienstleistung, Dienst, Service	
1A	**to join** [dʒɔɪn]	beitreten, mitmachen	He joined a fitness club.
	billion [ˈbɪljən]	Milliarde	
	billionth [ˈbɪljənθ]	milliardste / r / s	
	million [ˈmɪljən]	Million	
	user [ˈjuːzə]	Nutzer / in	
1B	**cheat sheet** [ˈtʃiːt ʃiːt]	Spickzettel	
	above [əˈbʌv]	oben(stehend)	above ↔ below
1C	**to name** [neɪm]	nennen, benennen	Can you name all the planets?
	to follow [ˈfɒləʊ]	folgen	
	reason [ˈriːzn]	Grund, Begründung	What's the reason you don't like Facebook?
2A	**history** [ˈhɪstri]	Geschichte	
	sneakers [ˈsniːkəz]	Turnschuhe	
	flat [flæt]	flach	It's flat here. There are no hills.
	rubber [ˈrʌbə]	Gummi	
	sole [səʊl]	Sohle	
	canvas [ˈkænvəs]	Segeltuch	
	top [tɒp]	Oberteil	
	simple [ˈsɪmpl]	einfach	
	comfortable [ˈkʌmftəbl]	bequem	comfortable ↔ uncomfortable
	to sneak [sniːk]	schleichen	
	quietly [ˈkwaɪətli]	leise	
	village [ˈvɪlɪdʒ]	Dorf	village – town – city
	spikes [spaɪks]	Spikes	
	athlete [ˈæθliːt]	Sportler / in, Leichtathlet / in	! Aussprache
	Olympic Games [əˌlɪmpɪk ˈɡeɪmz]	Olympische Spiele	
	fashionable [ˈfæʃnəbl]	in Mode	fashionable → fashion
	hi-tech [ˈhaɪ tek]	technologisch fortgeschritten	
	air [eə]	Luft	The air in the mountains is clean.
	pair [peə]	Paar	a pair of shoes
2B	**article** [ˈɑːtɪkl]	Artikel	
2C	**regular** [ˈreɡjələ]	regelmäßig	
	irregular [ɪˈreɡjələ]	unregelmäßig	
2F	**simple past** [ˌsɪmpl ˈpɑːst]	einfache Vergangenheit	
3A	**public relations** [ˌpʌblɪk rɪˈleɪʃnz]	PR, Öffentlichkeitsarbeit	
	department [dɪˈpɑːtmənt]	Abteilung	It's a big company, so there are many different departments.
	original [əˈrɪdʒənl]	ursprünglich, original	I still have the original photo.
	to design [dɪˈzaɪn]	entwerfen, gestalten	
	can [kæn]	Dose	a can of sth
	China [ˈtʃaɪnə]	China	! Aussprache
	lady [ˈleɪdi]	Dame	
	gentleman [ˈdʒentlmən]	Herr	
	to invent [ɪnˈvent]	erfinden	Who invented the mobile phone?
	pharmacist [ˈfɑːməsɪst]	(AE:) Apotheker / in	
	Atlanta [ətˈlæntə]	*Hauptstadt Georgias*	
	Georgia [ˈdʒɔːdʒə]	*US-Bundesstaat*	
	assistant [əˈsɪstnt]	Helfer / in, Assistent / in	I couldn't do the job without my assistant.
	design [dɪˈzaɪn]	Entwurf, Gestaltung	
	businessman [ˈbɪznɪsmən]	Geschäftsmann	
	at first [ət ˈfɜːst]	zunächst, zuerst	At first they lost money, then it got better.
	Austria [ˈɒstriə]	Österreich	

4A	race [reɪs]	Rennen, Wettlauf	
4B	at the back [ət ðə 'bæk]	hinten	I like to sit at the back of the cinema.
	to feel (felt, felt) [fiːl, felt, felt]	(sich) fühlen; der Meinung sein, meinen, finden	Do you feel well?
	audience ['ɔːdiəns]	Publikum, Zuschauer	The audience laughed.
	cool [kuːl]	cool, dufte	
	item ['aɪtəm]	Artikel	There are 100 items on the list.
	to become (became, become) [bɪ'kʌm, bɪ'keɪm, bɪ'kʌm]	werden	When did you become so slim?
	way [weɪ]	Weg, Art (und Weise)	There are many ways to cook rice.
4C	fact [fækt]	Tatsache	
4E	both [bəʊθ]	beide/s	Meat or fish? – I like both.
	muesli ['mjuːzli]	Müsli	
	orange juice ['ɒrɪndʒ dʒuːs]	Orangensaft	
	text [tekst]	SMS	I can't talk now. I will text you.
4F	gym [dʒɪm]	Fitnessklub	
4G	to translate [trænsˈleɪt]	übersetzen	to translate → translation
5A	invention [ɪnˈvenʃn]	Erfindung	invention → to invent → inventor
	mobile phone [məʊbaɪl 'fəʊn]	Mobiltelefon, Handy	
	phone call ['fəʊn kɔːl]	Anruf, Telefongespräch	
	to produce [prəˈdjuːs]	produzieren, herstellen	They produce these tablets in China.
	commercial [kəˈmɜːʃl]	kommerziell	commercial → commerce
	text messaging ['tekst mesɪdʒɪŋ]	Versenden von SMS	
	camera ['kæmərə]	Kamera	
	to weigh [weɪ]	wiegen	How much do you weigh?
	gram [græm]	Gramm	
	kilogram ['kɪləgræm]	Kilogramm	
V4	scene [siːn]	Szene	
	to shoot (shot, shot) [ʃuːt, ʃɒt, ʃɒt]	schießen	They shot the film in North Africa.
	leg [leg]	Bein	
	blood [blʌd]	Blut	
	packet ['pækɪt]	Packung	
	hole [həʊl]	Loch	
	remote control [rɪˌməʊt kənˈtrəʊl]	Fernbedienung	
	to carry ['kæri]	tragen, mit sich führen	On his last trip he carried 25 kg on his back.
	transmitter [trænsˈmɪtə]	Sender	
	pocket ['pɒkɪt]	(Hosen-, Hemd-)Tasche	I lost my money. There's a hole in my pocket.
	director [dəˈrektə]	Regisseur/in	
	to stay [steɪ]	bleiben	I'll stay until the end of the film.
	next door [nekst 'dɔː]	nebenan	
	unfortunately [ʌnˈfɔːtʃənətli]	unglücklicherweise, leider	It's raining and unfortunately I don't have an umbrella.

Unit 5 Dos and don'ts at work

	dos and don'ts [ˌduːz ən ˈdəʊnts]	Dinge, die man tun und lassen sollte	
1A	rule [ruːl]	Vorschrift, Regel	Do you know the rules for the present continuous tense?
	dental assistant [ˌdentl əˈsɪstnt]	Zahnarzthelfer/in	
1B	must not ['mʌst nɒt]	nicht dürfen	You mustn't smoke indoors.
	to have to ['hæv tə]	müssen	You have to smoke outside.
	carefully ['keəfli]	vorsichtig, sorgfältig, gut	
	polite [pəˈlaɪt]	höflich	polite ↔ impolite
	rude [ruːd]	unhöflich, unverschämt	
	clean [kliːn]	sauber	I need a clean shirt for the party.
	hygiene ['haɪdʒiːn]	Hygiene, Sauberkeit	

	dirty ['dɜːti]	schmutzig	Hygiene is important in a restaurant. Nothing can be dirty.
	hard hat [ˌhɑːd 'hæt]	Helm	
2A	sign [saɪn]	Schild	There's a sign on the door.
	factory ['fæktri]	Fabrik	
	car park ['kɑː pɑːk]	Parkplatz, Parkhaus	
	construction site [kənˈstrʌkʃn saɪt]	Baustelle	It's just a construction site now but later it will be a beautiful building.
	smoking ['sməʊkɪŋ]	Rauchen	
	floor [flɔː]	Boden, Fußboden	There are carpets on the floor.
	electricity [ɪˌlekˈtrɪsəti]	Elektrizität, Strom	
	lorry ['lɒri]	Lkw	
	driver ['draɪvə]	Fahrer/in	
	bag [bæg]	Tasche, Reisetasche	I left my bag in the taxi!
	fire ['faɪə]	Feuer	
	to transport [trænˈspɔːt]	transportieren, befördern	to transport → transportation
	heavy ['hevi]	schwer	heavy ↔ light
	cell phone ['sel fəʊn]	(AE:) Handy	
	face [feɪs]	Gesicht	With those dark glasses I can't see your face.
	face shield ['feɪs ʃiːld]	Gesichtsschutz, Schutzmaske	
	no-smoking [ˌnəʊ 'sməʊkɪŋ]	Nichtraucher-	
	no-smoking area [ˌnəʊ 'sməʊkɪŋ eriə]	Nichtraucherbereich	
	no parking [ˌnəʊ 'pɑːkɪŋ]	Parken verboten	
	danger ['deɪndʒə]	Gefahr	danger → dangerous
	volt [vɒlt]	Volt	
	caution [kɔːʃn]	Vorsicht	! Aussprache
	fork-lift truck ['fɔːk lɪft trʌk]	Gabelstapler	
	Keep out! [kiːp 'aʊt]	Betreten verboten!	
	wet [wet]	nass, feucht	wet ↔ dry
	case [keɪs]	Fall	
	in case of fire [ɪn ˌkeɪs əf 'faɪə]	im Brandfall	
	to break (broke, broken) [breɪk, brəʊk, 'brəʊkən]	zerbrechen, kaputtmachen, einschlagen	The glass fell and broke.
	goggles ['gɒglz]	Schutzbrille	He wears goggles in the swimming pool.
	ear protectors [ɪə prəˈtektəz]	Gehörschutz	
	security [sɪˈkjʊərəti]	Sicherheit	
	property ['prɒpəti]	Eigentum	Houses and flats are property.
	unattended [ˌʌnəˈtendɪd]	unbeaufsichtigt	Parents must not leave their children unattended.
	reception [rɪˈsepʃn]	Rezeption	
2C	to smoke [sməʊk]	rauchen	
	to park [pɑːk]	parken	
2D	to explain [ɪkˈspleɪn]	erklären, erläutern	Can you explain how it works?
	casual ['kæʒuəl]	leger, ungezwungen	The new boss is very relaxed and casual.
	formal ['fɔːml]	formell, förmlich	
	suit [suːt]	Anzug	Men and women wear suits.
	skirt [skɜːt]	Rock	
3	conflict ['kɒnflɪkt]	Streit, Konflikt	When people don't agree about something that may be conflict.
	news story ['njuːz stɔːri]	(aktueller) Artikel, Reportage	
	workplace ['wɜːkpleɪs]	Arbeitsplatz	
	in the workplace [ɪn ðə 'wɜːkpleɪs]	am Arbeitsplatz	
	task [tɑːsk]	Aufgabe	
	dental practice ['dentl præktɪs]	Zahnarztpraxis	
	reception desk [rɪˈsepʃn desk]	Empfang, Anmeldung	
	to answer the phone [ˌɑːnsə ðə 'fəʊn]	ans Telefon gehen, Anrufe entgegennehmen	

	appointment [əˈpɔɪntmənt]	Termin	I have a dental appointment at 9 am.
	and so on [ənd ˌsəʊ ˈɒn]	uns so weiter	
	to share [ʃeə]	(sich etw) teilen	
	dentist [ˈdentɪst]	Zahnarzt / -ärztin	
	cash [kæʃ]	Bargeld	Do you want cash or a cheque?
	to refuse [rɪˈfjuːz]	sich weigern	She is so angry that she refuses to see me.
	generally [ˈdʒenrəli]	im Allgemeinen, eigentlich	Generally, people in the office are very friendly.
	national [ˈnæʃnl]	landesweit, national	
	chain [tʃeɪn]	Kette	They have a chain of shops all over the country.
	angry [ˈæŋgri]	böse, wütend, verärgert	
	to get angry [ˈget æŋgri]	sich aufregen, sich ärgern	He got angry when I told him the truth.
	unhappy [ˌʌnˈhæpi]	unzufrieden, unglücklich	
	manager [ˈmænɪdʒə]	Geschäftsführer / in	
	others [ˈʌðəz]	die anderen, andere	Only two people came. The others were busy.
	on the other hand [ˌɒn ðɪ ˈʌðə hænd]	dagegen, andererseits	I have work to do. On the other hand, the weather is so nice.
	to clean [kliːn]	säubern, reinigen, putzen	
	to move sth around [ˌmuːv əˈraʊnd]	etw herumtragen, etw herumschleppen	I want to move the furniture in my room around.
3B	**according to** [əˈkɔːdɪŋ tə]	gemäß, zufolge, nach	
	feeling [ˈfiːlɪŋ]	Gefühl, Meinung, Ansicht	I'm afraid to tell her my true feelings.
	to solve [sɒlv]	lösen	I'm sure we can solve the problem.
	boss [bɒs]	Chef / in	
	head office [ˌhed ˈɒfɪs]	(Firmen-)Zentrale	
	probably [ˈprɒbəbli]	wahrscheinlich	He's probably late because of the traffic.
	situation [ˌsɪtjuˈeɪʃn]	Situation, Lage	
	to put up with sth [ˌpʊt ˈʌp wɪð]	etw hinnehmen, sich etw gefallen lassen	There are some things I can't put up with. I'm going!
	discussion [dɪsˈkʌʃn]	Diskussion	
4A	**nowadays** [ˈnaʊədeɪz]	heutzutage, heute	Nowadays everybody has a smartphone.
	distance [ˈdɪstəns]	Entfernung, Strecke	
4B	**office worker** [ˈɒfɪs wɜːkə]	Büroangestellte / r	
	tie [taɪ]	Krawatte	
	Coney Island [ˌkəʊni ˈaɪlənd]	südl. Zipfel von Brooklyn mit Strand und Vergnügungsparks	
	to relax [rɪˈlæks]	sich ausruhen, sich entspannen	to relax → relaxation
	to enjoy sth [ɪnˈdʒɔɪ]	etw genießen	I really enjoyed the party.
4C	**lottery** [ˈlɒtəri]	Lotto, Lotterie	
	meeting [ˈmiːtɪŋ]	Sitzung, Besprechung, Treffen	
	punctually [ˈpʌŋktʃuəli]	pünktlich	John always arrives at meetings punctually.
	forbidden [fəˈbɪdn]	verboten	
	pupil [ˈpjuːpl]	Schüler / in	
	immediately [iˈmiːdiətli]	unverzüglich, sofort	His dad had an accident. He had to leave immediately.
4D	**Birmingham** [ˈbɜːmɪŋəm]	zweitgrößte Stadt Großbritanniens	
	work placement [ˈwɜːk pleɪsmənt]	Praktikum	
	description [dɪˈskrɪpʃn]	Beschreibung	description → to describe
	necessary [ˈnesəsri]	nötig, notwendig	Don't bring flowers. They are not necessary.
	to dress [dres]	sich kleiden	
	smartly [ˈsmɑːtli]	schick, elegant	He always dresses casually.
	punctual [ˈpʌŋktʃʊəl]	pünktlich	
	to turn off [ˌtɜːn ˈɒf]	ausschalten	to turn off ↔ to turn on
	call [kɔːl]	Anruf, Telefongespräch	
	to receive [rɪˈsiːv]	empfangen, erhalten	to receive ↔ to send
	to ring sb (rang, rung) [rɪŋ, ræŋ, rʌŋ]	klingeln, läuten; jdn anrufen	I will ring her in the morning.
4F	**road sign** [ˈrəʊd saɪn]	Straßenschild, Verkehrsschild	

	traffic lights ['træfɪk ˌlaɪts]	Ampel	The traffic lights were red.
	speed [spiːd]	Geschwindigkeit	
	speed limit ['spiːd lɪmɪt]	Geschwindigkeitsbegrenzung	
	per [pə, pɜː]	pro	
	to be allowed to do sth [bi əˌlaʊd tə 'duː]	etw tun dürfen	You aren't allowed to smoke in the cinema.
4G	goods [gʊdz]	Güter, Waren	They receive the goods from all over Europe.
V5	personal assistant [ˌpɜːsnl əˈsɪstənt]	persönliche / r Referent / in, Chefsekretär / in	

Unit 6 Success stories

	success [sək'ses]	Erfolg	His first song was a great success.
	patio ['pætiəʊ]	Terrasse	There's a table outside on the patio.
1A	to be born [bi 'bɔːn]	geboren werden	
	Poland ['pəʊlənd]	Polen	
	to move to [muːv]	nach … ziehen	They left and moved to a new town.
	plumber ['plʌmə]	Klempner / in	'b' wird nicht ausgesprochen.
	own [əʊn]	eigen	my / your / his … own
	building firm ['bɪldɪŋ fɜːm]	Bauunternehmen	
	employee [ɪm'plɔɪiː]	Angestellte / r	
	successful [sək'sesfl]	erfolgreich	successful at sth
1B	local ['ləʊkl]	Lokal-, Orts-, örtlich	! Aussprache
	diagram ['daɪəgræm]	Grafik, Schaubild, Diagramm; auch: Wohnungsgrundriss	! Betonung
2A	to be no good [ˌbi nəʊ 'gʊd]	nichts taugen	good at sth
	at the top [ət ðə 'tɒp]	oben	top ↔ bottom
	south-east [ˌsaʊθ'iːst]	Südosten	
	pub [pʌb]	Kneipe	a place where people drink and talk to friends
	dyslexic [dɪs'leksɪk]	legasthenisch	
	on TV [ɒn ˌtiː'viː]	im Fernsehen	
	show [ʃəʊ]	(TV-)Sendung, Serie	
	unsuccessful [ˌʌnsək'sesfl]	erfolglos	unsuccessful ↔ successful
	to open ['əʊpən]	eröffnen	
	normal ['nɔːml]	normal, gewöhnlich	! Aussprache
	unemployed [ˌʌnɪm'plɔɪd]	arbeitslos	unemployed → to employ → employee
	to train sb [treɪn]	jdn ausbilden	They trained her to work in our call centre.
	to marry ['mæri]	heiraten	married to sb
2E	present perfect [ˌpreznt 'pɜːfɪkt]	Perfekt	
3B	news [njuːz]	Nachrichten	(immer Singular:) The news is …
	cookery ['kʊkəri]	Kochen	cookery → to cook → a cook
	cookery course ['kʊkəri kɔːs]	Kochkurs	
3D	piece [piːs]	Stück	a piece of paper
	clothing ['kləʊðɪŋ]	Kleidung	
4D	police officer [pə'liːs ɒfɪsə]	Polizeibeamte / r	
	love [lʌv]	Liebe	
	tense [tens]	Zeit, Zeitform	
4E	leisure ['leʒə]	Freizeit	In his leisure time he plays a lot of tennis.
4F	world championship [ˌwɜːld 'tʃæmpiənʃɪp]	Weltmeisterschaft	
	world champion [ˌwɜːld 'tʃæmpiən]	Weltmeister / in	
	junior high school [ˌdʒuːniə 'haɪ skuːl]	Mittelschule	
	professional [prə'feʃənl]	professionell, berufsmäßig	
	to take part in [ˌteɪk 'pɑːt ɪn]	teilnehmen an	She's taken part in competitions all over the world.
	pro [prəʊ]	Profi	
	Japan [dʒə'pæn]	Japan	

| Grammar summary | Skills files |  **Vocabulary** |

	journalist [ˈdʒɜːnəlɪst]	Journalist / in	
	headline [ˈhedlaɪn]	Überschrift, Schlagzeile	
5A	**screen name** [ˈskriːn neɪm]	Benutzername, Username	
	to continue [kənˈtɪnjuː]	fortsetzen, fortführen	Don't stop talking. Please continue.

Unit 7 Looking ahead

	to look ahead [ˌlʊk əˈhed]	vorausschauen	Look ahead, don't look behind.
1A	**still** [stɪl]	noch (immer)	They are still friends.
	in 10 years [ɪn ten ˈjɪəz]	in / nach 10 Jahren	10 years later
1C	**vacation** [vəˈkeɪʃn]	(AE:) Ferien	(BE:) holidays
	to leave home [ˌliːv ˈhəʊm]	von zu Hause ausziehen	
	mom [mɒm]	(AE:) Mama	(BE:) mum
	to look for [ˈlʊk fə]	suchen	to look for, to look at, to look after
2A	**Denton** [ˈdentən]	Stadt in Texas	
	elevator [ˈnɔːθ ˌəv]	nördlich von	north ↔ south
	Dallas [ˈdæləs]	Hauptstadt von Texas	
	Texas [ˈteksəs]	US-Bundesstaat	
	different [ˈdɪfrənt]	unterschiedlich, anders	different ↔ the same
2D	**wages** [ˈweɪdʒɪz]	Lohn	They pay good wages.
	nervous [ˈnɜːvəs]	nervös, aufgeregt	! Betonung
3A	**studio apartment** [ˌstjuːdiəʊ əˈpɑːtmənt]	Einzimmerwohnung, Appartement	(BE:) studio flat
	bedside cabinet [ˈbedsaɪd kæbɪnət]	Nachttisch	bedside cupboard, bedside lamp
	coffee table [ˈkɒfi teɪbl]	Couchtisch	The coffee table is next to the sofa.
	computer desk [kəmˈpjuːtə desk]	Computertisch	
	dining table [ˈdaɪnɪŋ teɪbl]	Esstisch	Our dining table is in the living room.
	chair [tʃeə]	Stuhl	
	electric kettle [ɪˈlektrɪk ketl]	elektrischer Wasserkocher	You make water hot with an electric kettle.
	houseplant [ˈhaʊsplɑːnt]	Zimmerpflanze	
	lamp [læmp]	Lampe	
	microwave [ˈmaɪkrəʊweɪv]	Mikrowelle	You can't cook a meal in the microwave, but you can warm something up.
	mirror [ˈmɪrə]	Spiegel	He can see himself in the mirror.
	pinboard [ˈpɪnbɔːd]	Pinnwand	There are lots of post-its on the pinboard.
	rug [rʌg]	Teppich, Vorleger	
	toaster [ˈtəʊstə]	Toaster	toaster → to toast
	sofa [ˈsəʊfə]	Sofa	
	wall bracket [wɔːl ˈbrækɪt]	Wandhalterung	You need a bracket to fix your TV on the wall.
	wall clock [wɔːl ˈklɒk]	Wanduhr	a clock on the wall
3B	**to paint sth** [peɪnt]	anstreichen, malen	He painted one wall in his room pink.
	fridge [frɪdʒ]	Kühlschrank	refrigerator
	cupboard [ˈkʌbəd]	Küchenschrank	
	to be sure [ʃʊə]	sicher sein	sure ↔ unsure
3C	**to imagine** [ɪˈmædʒɪn]	sich vorstellen	Can you imagine the end of the story?
	furniture [ˈfɜːnɪtʃə]	Möbel	(kein Plural!) bed, chair, table etc.
	to present [prɪˈzent]	vorführen, präsentieren	! Betonung to present → present → presentation
	shower [ˈʃaʊə]	Dusche	Did you have a bath or a shower?
	washbasin [ˈwɒʃbeɪsn]	Waschbecken	There are two washbasins in the bathroom.
	toilet [ˈtɔɪlət]	Toilette	
	wardrobe [ˈwɔːdrəʊb]	Kleiderschrank	You keep your clothes in a wardrobe.
	entrance [ˈentrəns]	Eingang	entrance → to enter
	cooker [ˈkʊkə]	Herd	cooker → to cook → cookery
	sink [sɪŋk]	Spüle	
4A	**occupation** [ˌɒkjəˈpeɪʃn]	Beschäftigung, Tätigkeit	occupation → to occupy
	volunteer [ˌvɒlənˈtɪə]	Freiwillige / r	volunteer → voluntary

	summer camp ['sʌmə ˌkæmp]	Sommerferienlager	
	dormitory ['dɔ:mɪtəri]	(AE:) Studentenwohnheim	(BE:) students' hall A dormitory is usually cheaper than a studio apartment.
	lifeguard ['laɪfgɑ:d]	Rettungsschwimmer/in	
	sort (of) [sɔ:t]	Art, Sorte	kind (of)
4C	**movie** ['mu:vi]	(AE:) Film	(BE:) film
	fascinating ['fæsɪneɪtɪŋ]	faszinierend	
	rubbish ['rʌbɪʃ]	Müll	(kein Plural!) Put the rubbish into the rubbish bin, please.
4F	**quite** [kwaɪt]	ziemlich	She speaks English quite well.
V7	**column** ['kɒləm]	(Text-)Spalte	

| Grammar summary | Skills files | **Vocabulary**

Alphabetisches Vokabular

A
above oben(stehend) 57
access Zugang, Zugriff 11
accident Unfall 46
according to gemäß, zufolge, nach 73
actor Schauspieler 12
adjective Adjektiv 48
administration Verwaltung 25
air Luft 58
airport Flughafen 52
album Album, CD, Schallplatte 13
almost fast, beinah 24
and so on uns so weiter 72
angry böse, wütend, verärgert 72
to answer the phone ans Telefon gehen, Anrufe entgegennehmen 72
antivirus Antivirus- 51
apartment (AE:) Wohnung 14
appointment Termin 72
a quarter to (Uhrzeit:) Viertel vor 14
area Gebiet 25
around ungefähr, zirka 34
around the world auf der ganzen Welt 20
art Kunst, Grafik 25
article Artikel 59
assistant Helfer/in, Assistent/in 60
astronaut Astronaut/in 27
at first zunächst, zuerst 60
at the back hinten 62
at the top oben 82
at work bei der Arbeit 17
athlete Sportler/in, Leichtathlet/in 58
athletics Leichtathletik 22
audience Publikum, Zuschauer 62
automotive mechanics Kraftfahrzeugmechanik 25

B
back Rücken 12
backpacker Rucksacktourist/in 16
bag Tasche, Reisetasche 70
to bake backen 45
barista Barista, Kaffeezubereiter/in in Espressobar 48
barman Barkeeper 36
battery Batterie, Akku 37
to be allowed to do sth etw tun dürfen 76
to be born geboren werden 81
to be called heißen 9
to be keen on sth von etw begeistert/angetan sein 47
to be no good nichts taugen 82
to be sure sicher sein 96
bean Bohne 16
beauty Schönheit, Kosmetik 25
to become (became, become) werden 62
bedside cabinet Nachttisch 96
beer Bier 37
before bevor 29
to belong gehören 38
belt Gürtel 44
the best thing of all das Beste von allem 48
between zwischen 25
billion Milliarde 57
billionth milliardste/r/s 57
blood Blut 65
body Körper 12
to book reservieren, buchen 16
boss Chef/in 73
both beide/s 64
bottom Ende, (Seite:) Fuß 28
box Kasten, Kästchen 54
break Pause 22
to break (broke, broken) zerbrechen, kaputtmachen, einschlagen 71
brilliant großartig, hervorragend 47
Brits (die) Briten 53
brochure Prospekt, Broschüre 10
building firm Bauunternehmen 81
burger Burger 51
bus driver Busfahrer/in 16
business administration Betriebswirtschaftslehre 25
business course Betriebswirtschaftslehrgang 22
businessman Geschäftsmann 60
busy (viel)beschäftigt 36
by far bei Weitem 51
bye tschüs 10

C
to call anrufen 16
call Anruf, Telefongespräch 75
camera Kamera 65
can Dose 60
canoeing Kanufahren 10
canvas Segeltuch 58
capital (city) Hauptstadt 17
capital letter Großbuchstabe 29
car park Parkplatz, Parkhaus 70
career Beruf, Laufbahn, Karriere 33
careful vorsichtig 37
carefully vorsichtig, sorgfältig, gut 69
carrot Karotte, Möhre 16
to carry tragen, mit sich führen 65
case Fall 71
cash Bargeld 72
casual leger, ungezwungen 71
caution Vorsicht 71
celeb Promi 12
celebrity Prominente/r 12
cell phone (AE:) Handy 70
certainly gewiss, sicherlich 16
chain Kette 72
chair Stuhl 96
cheat sheet Spickzettel 57
to check überprüfen, kontrollieren 10
cheesecake Käsekuchen 49
chef Koch/Köchin 40
child care Kinderbetreuung 25
to choose (chose, chosen) wählen, auswählen, aussuchen 19
classroom Klassenzimmer 29
clean sauber 69
to clean säubern, reinigen, putzen 72
clothes Kleidung 51
clothing Kleidung 85
coffee table Couchtisch 96
colleague Kollege/Kollegin 40
college Hochschule, Berufsbildende Schule, Universität 20
column (Text-)Spalte 101
comfortable bequem 58
commercial kommerziell 65
community Gemeinde 20
community college (USA:) College, das ein Zweijahresstudium anbietet, hauptsächlich für Studenten aus der Gegend 20
company Unternehmen, Firma 14
comparative Komparativ 48
to compare vergleichen 29
competition Wettbewerb 29
to complete vervollständigen 10
to complete ausfüllen 41
computer desk Computertisch 96
conflict Streit, Konflikt 72
construction Baugewerbe, Bauwesen 25
construction site Baustelle 70
construction worker Bauarbeiter/in 8
to contact sich in Verbindung setzen mit 11
to continue fortsetzen, fortführen 89
conversation Gespräch, Unterhaltung 16
cook Koch/Köchin 17
cooker Herd 97
cookery Kochen 84
cookery course Kochkurs 84
cookie (AE:) Keks, Plätzchen 49
cool cool, dufte 62
course Kurs, Lehrgang 21
credit etwa: Leistungspunkte 25
credit card Kreditkarte 16
crocodile Krokodil 36
crown Krone 17
cupboard Küchenschrank 96
customer Kunde/Kundin 37

to cut (cut, cut) schneiden 34
to cut grass Rasen mähen 34
cycle ride Fahrradfahrt 46
cycling Fahrradfahren 10

D

danger Gefahr 71
to decide entscheiden 38
decorator Maler/in, Tapezierer/in 9
to deliver (aus)liefern, *(Post:)* austragen 36
dental assistant Zahnarzthelfer/in 69
dental practice Zahnarztpraxis 72
dentist Zahnarzt/-ärztin 72
department Abteilung 60
to depend on abhängen von, ankommen auf 28
to describe beschreiben 40
description Beschreibung 75
design Gestaltung, Design 25
to design entwerfen, gestalten 60
design Entwurf, Gestaltung 60
details Einzelheiten, Angaben 25
diagram Grafik, Schaubild, Diagramm; auch: Wohnungsgrundriss 81
diet Ernährung; Diät 32
different unterschiedlich, anders 94
dining room Esszimmer, Speisesaal 10
dining table Esstisch 96
director Regisseur/in 65
dirty schmutzig 69
discussion Diskussion 73
dislike Abneigung 47
distance Entfernung, Strecke 74
doctor Arzt, Ärztin 9
doctor's receptionist Sprechstundenhilfe 9
dormitory *(AE:)* Studentenwohnheim 98
dos and don'ts Dinge, die man tun und lassen sollte 68
double room Doppelzimmer 16
to dress sich kleiden 75
to drive (drove, driven) fahren 39
driver Fahrer/in 70
driving test Führerschein 46
dyslexic legasthenisch 82

E

each jede/r/s 34
ear protectors Gehörschutz 71
to earn verdienen 48
eastern östlich, Ost- 37
education Bildung, Ausbildung 44
electric kettle elektrischer Wasserkocher 16
electrical elektrisch 16
electrician Elektriker/in 28
electricity Elektrizität, Strom 70
electronics Elektronik 25
to email eine E-Mail schreiben 25

employee Angestellte/r 81
engine Motor 16
to enjoy sth etw genießen 74
enough genug, genügend 25
entrance Eingang 97
entry Zugang 6
etc. usw. 11
euro Euro 16
even sogar, noch 25
everyone jeder, alle 25
exchange Austausch 20
exciting aufregend, spannend 52
exercise machine Fitnessgerät 32
to explain erklären, erläutern 71
extremely äußerst 27

F

face Gesicht 70
face shield Gesichtsschutz, Schutzmaske 70
facilities Einrichtung(en), Räumlichkeiten, Ausstattung 10
fact Tatsache 63
factory Fabrik 70
famous berühmt 52
fascinating faszinierend 100
fashion Mode 14
fashionable in Mode 58
FE college Berufsschule 45
to feel (felt, felt) (sich) fühlen 62
feeling Gefühl, Meinung, Ansicht 73
fire Feuer 70
first aid Erste Hilfe 46
fit fit, gesund 32
to fit sth around sth um etw herum anordnen 48
fitness club Fitnessklub 15
fitness trainer Fitnesstrainer 32
flat flach 58
floor Boden, Fußboden 70
to flow fließen 23
fly Mücke 37
folks Leute 36
to follow folgen 57
footballer Fußballspieler/in 12
forbidden verboten 74
foreground Vordergrund 40
fork-lift truck Gabelstapler 71
formal formell, förmlich 71
France Frankreich 12
free time Freizeit 44
fridge Kühlschrank 96
fries *(AE:)* Pommes 16
from around the world aus der ganzen Welt 17
full-time Ganztags-, Vollzeit- 22
furniture Möbel 97

G

gallery Galerie 29
gardener Gärtner/in 34

garlic Knoblauch 40
G'day *(AustrE:)* Guten Tag! 8
generally im Allgemeinen, eigentlich 72
gentleman Herr 60
to get angry sich aufregen, sich ärgern 72
to get back to sich melden bei 20
to get ready sich vorbereiten, sich fertig machen 40
to get to know kennen lernen 20
to go off losgehen 16
to go on holiday (to) Urlaub machen (in) 10
goggles Schutzbrille 71
goods Güter, Waren 76
gram Gramm 65
graph Diagramm 53
group Gruppe 29
gym Fitnessklub 47
gym Fitnessklub 64

H

hairdresser Friseur/in 25
hairdressing salon Friseursalon 37
to hang out with (hung, hung) mit jdm abhängen, sich mit jdm rumtreiben 22
hard hat Helm 69
to have to müssen 69
head office (Firmen-)Zentrale 73
headline Überschrift, Schlagzeile 88
health Gesundheit, Gesundheitswesen 25
healthy gesund, gesundheitsfördernd 32
heavy schwer 70
Here you go. Hier, bitte sehr. 37
high school Oberschule 24
Highway Code Straßenverkehrsordnung 46
history Geschichte 58
hi-tech technologisch fortgeschritten 58
to hold (held, held) halten, festhalten 37
hole Loch 65
to hope hoffen 20
horse Pferd 19
hostel Herberge 10
hostel warden Herbergsvater/-mutter 10
hours Arbeitszeiten 32
houseplant Zimmerpflanze 96
to hunt jagen 37
hunter Jäger 36
hygiene Hygiene, Sauberkeit 69

I

ill krank 38
to imagine sich etw vorstellen 18
to imagine sich vorstellen 97
immediately unverzüglich, sofort 74

| Grammar summary | Skills files | **Vocabulary**

in case of fire im Brandfall 71
in fact eigentlich, um genau zu sein 36
in 10 years in / nach 10 Jahren
in the workplace am Arbeitsplatz 72
information Angaben, Information(en) 27
information technology Informationstechnologie 25
inline skates Inline-Skates 13
inside drinnen 32
international international 20
to interview interviewen 36
to invent erfinden 60
invention Erfindung 65
irregular unregelmäßig 59
It depends. Kommt darauf an. 28
item Artikel 62

J
jewellery Schmuck 47
to jog joggen 14
to join beitreten, mitmachen 57
journalist Journalist / in 88
junior high school Mittelschule 88
Just a minute! Einen Moment! 16

K
to keep fit (kept, kept) sich fit halten 32
Keep out! Betreten verboten! 71
to keep still ruhig halten 37
kilo Kilo 37
kilogram Kilogramm 65
kitchen Küche 40

L
lady Dame 60
lamb Lamm 40
lamp Lampe 96
laptop Laptop, Notebook 13
large ausgedehnt, großflächig 52
to last dauern 24
to leave (left, left) hinterlassen, dalassen 20
to leave home von zu Hause ausziehen 93
leg Bein 65
leisure Freizeit 87
life Leben 37
lifeguard Rettungsschwimmer / in 98
lifestyle Lebensweise 32
to lift heben, hochheben 39
likes Vorlieben 47
litre Liter 37
local Lokal-, Orts-, örtlich 81
to look after sich kümmern um, pflegen 34
to look ahead vorausschauen 92
to look for suchen 93
to look forward to doing sth sich auf etw freuen 16

lorry Lkw 70
lottery Lotto, Lotterie 74
love Liebe 87
lunch break Mittagspause 22
lyrics Liedtext, Songtext 46

M
mail Post 36
main Haupt- 11
main street Hauptstraße 11
mall Einkaufszentrum 26
manager Geschäftsführer / in 72
marketing company Vertriebsgesellschaft 22
married to verheiratet mit 17
to marry heiraten 82
to match zuordnen 14
match Spiel 51
maybe vielleicht 16
meat Fleisch 40
mechanic Mechaniker / in 16
mechanical mechanisch 34
media Medien 25
medical centre Klinikum 46
medium rare (Steak:) medium 16
meeting Sitzung, Besprechung, Treffen 74
menu Speisekarte 16
message Nachricht, Mitteilung 20
microwave Mikrowelle 96
million Million 57
mirror Spiegel 96
missing fehlend 14
mistake Fehler, Irrtum 53
mobile phone Mobiltelefon, Handy 65
model Muster, Vorlage 41
mom (AE:) Mama 93
most of the time meistens 16
motor bike Motorrad 13
mountain Berg 10
to move sth around etw herumtragen, etw herumschleppen 72
to move to nach ... ziehen 81
movie (AE:) Film 99
movie theater (AE:) Kino 11
much viel 10
muesli Müsli 64
muffin Muffin, Törtchen 49
musical instrument Musikinstrument 13
musician Musiker / in 12
must not nicht dürfen 69

N
to name nennen, benennen 57
national landesweit, national 72
native speaker Muttersprachler / in 8
nature Natur 34
necessary nötig, notwendig 75
to need brauchen, benötigen 25
negative verneinend, negativ 27

nervous nervös, aufgeregt 95
networking Netzwerk(-) 14
news Nachrichten 84
news story (aktueller) Artikel, Reportage 72
newspaper Zeitung 37
next door nebenan 65
next to neben 18
no parking Parken verboten 71
No way! Nie im Leben! Auf gar keinen Fall! 13
normal normal, gewöhnlich 82
normally üblicherweise, normalerweise 26
north of nördlich von 94
northern nördlich, Nord- 37
no-smoking Nichtraucher- 71
no-smoking area Nichtraucherbereich 71
to note down notieren, aufschreiben 12
noticeboard Schwarzes Brett 29
nowadays heutzutage, heute 74
nurse Krankenschwester, Krankenpfleger 8
nursery assistant Hilfslehrerin im Kindergarten 35
nursery (school) Kindergarten 38

O
occupation Beschäftigung, Tätigkeit 98
to offer bieten, anbieten 24
office worker Büroangestellte / r 74
Olympic Games Olympische Spiele 58
on the other hand dagegen, andererseits 72
on the phone am Telefon 10
on the way unterwegs 29
on TV im Fernsehen 82
once einmal 12
one day eines Tages 24
to open eröffnen 82
orange juice Orangensaft 64
to order bestellen 16
order Reihenfolge 36
to organise organisieren 20
original ursprünglich, original 60
others die anderen, andere 72
ouch! au! 37
outside draußen 33
over über 25
over there dort drüben 40
own eigen 81

P
package Paket 36
packet Packung 65
to paint sth anstreichen, malen 96
painter Maler / in, Anstreicher / in 9
pair Paar 58
to park parken 71
particularly vor allem, insbesondere 20

part-time Halbtags-, Teilzeit- 28
part-time job Teilzeitjob 48
past (Uhrzeit:) nach 14
patio Terrasse 80
pea Erbse 16
per pro 76
personal persönlich 32
personal assistant persönliche / r Referent / in, Chefsekretär / in 77
personal trainer (persönlicher) Fitnesstrainer 32
pharmacist *(AE:)* Apotheker / in 60
pharmacy *(AE:)* Apotheke 11
to phone anrufen, telefonieren 37
phone call Anruf, Telefongespräch 65
photographer Fotograf / in 46
phrase Wendung, Ausdruck 18
piano Klavier 12
piece Stück 85
pinboard Pinnwand 96
place Ort, Platz, Stelle
planet Planet 27
plant Pflanze 34
platform Plattform 20
plumber Klempner / in 81
pocket (Hosen-, Hemd-)Tasche 65
to point to zeigen auf 14
police officer Polizeibeamte / r 87
polite höflich 69
popular beliebt 46
population Bevölkerung, Einwohnerzahl 37
to post posten, einen Beitrag schreiben 48
post office Postamt 11
poster Plakat 13
postman Postbote 36
postwoman Postbotin 41
practical praktisch, sinnvoll, vernünftig 28
to prepare zubereiten, kochen 40
to present vorführen, präsentieren 97
present continuous Verlaufsform des Präsens 38
present perfect Perfekt 83
private privat, Privat- 27
prize Gewinn, Preis 29
pro Profi 88
probably wahrscheinlich 73
to produce produzieren, herstellen 65
product Produkt 56
professional professionell, berufsmäßig 88
profile Profil, Beschreibung, Porträt 33
project Projekt 20
property Eigentum 71
pub Kneipe 82
public relations PR, Öffentlichkeitsarbeit 60
punctual pünktlich 75
punctually pünktlich 74

pupil Schüler / in 74
to put up with sth etw hinnehmen, sich etw gefallen lassen 73

Q
queen Königin 52
questionnaire Fragebogen 13
quiet ruhig, still 38
quietly leise 58
quite ziemlich 100

R
race Rennen, Wettlauf 62
radio station Radiosender 26
ready bereit, fertig 16
real wirklich, ziemlich, *hier:* sehr 36
really wirklich, ziemlich, hier: sehr 47
reason Grund, Begründung 57
to receive empfangen, erhalten 75
reception Rezeption 71
reception desk Empfang, Anmeldung 72
receptionist Empfangsdame, -mitarbeiter 9
record Rekord 51
to refuse sich weigern 72
regular regelmäßig 59
regularly regelmäßig 29
to relax sich ausruhen, sich entspannen 74
remote control Fernbedienung 65
to repair reparieren 34
to report to (jdm) Bericht erstatten 29
to reserve reservieren 16
result Ergebnis 53
retail services Einzelhandel 25
right now im Augenblick, gerade 33
to ring sb (rang, rung) klingeln, läuten 75
road sign Straßenschild, Verkehrsschild 76
rubber Gummi 58
rubbish Müll 100
rude unhöflich, unverschämt 69
rug Teppich, Vorleger 96
rule Vorschrift, Regel 69

S
salad Salat 51
salon (Friseur-, Kosmetik-)Salon 35
sauce Soße 40
to say hello to sb jdn begrüßen 14
scene Szene 65
scooter Motorroller 13
screen name Benutzername, Username 89
to search suchen, durchsuchen 20
security Sicherheit 71
See you later. Bis dann! 37
to serve *(Kunden)* bedienen, *(Speisen)* servieren 37

to service warten 34
service Dienstleistung, Dienst, Service 56
to share (sich etw) teilen 72
sheep Schaf, Schafe 37
shoe shop Schuhgeschäft 16
to shoot (shot, shot) schießen 65
shop assistant Verkäufer / in 16
shorts kurze Hosen 40
should sollte / n 16
show (TV-)Sendung, Serie 82
to show sb round jdn herumführen 40
shower Dusche 97
side Seite 12
sight Sehenswürdigkeit 29
sign Schild 70
simple einfach 58
simple past einfache Vergangenheit 59
simple present einfaches Präsens 26
since seit 29
singer Sänger / in 12
single room Einzelzimmer 16
sink Spüle 97
sir mein Herr 16
to sit down sich (hin)setzen 16
site Website 14
situation Situation, Lage 73
size Größe 16
skirt Rock 71
smartly schick, elegant 75
to smoke rauchen 71
smoking Rauchen 70
to sneak schleichen 58
sneakers Turnschuhe 58
social sozial 14
social networking site soziales Netzwerk 45
social work Sozialarbeit 25
sofa Sofa 96
sole Sohle 58
to solve lösen 73
sort (of) Art, Sorte 98
south-east Südosten 82
southern südlich, Süd- 37
speaking am Apparat 10
speed Geschwindigkeit 76
speed limit Geschwindigkeitsbegrenzung 76
spelling Schreibweise, Rechtschreibung 39
spikes Spikes 58
sports centre Sportzentrum 32
sportspeople Sportler 12
stadium Stadion 33
star Star 12
to start starten 16
state Staat, Bundesstaat 23
to stay bleiben 65
steak Steak 16
still noch (immer) 93

Grammar summary | Skills files | **Vocabulary**

to stop anhalten, stehen bleiben, *(Motor:)* ausgehen 16
stopover Zwischenaufenthalt, Zwischenstation 29
strange seltsam, komisch 28
studio apartment Einzimmerwohnung, Appartement 96
subject Fach; Thema 25
subway *(AE:)* U-Bahn 14
success Erfolg 80
successful erfolgreich 81
suit Anzug 71
summer camp Sommerferienlager 98
superlative Superlativ 48
supper Abendessen 14
to surf surfen 17
survey Umfrage 53
sweet süß 49
swimming pool Schwimmbad 11
system System 52

T

to take it in turns sich abwechseln 7
to take off *(Flugzeug:)* starten, abheben 40
to take part in teilnehmen an 88
task Aufgabe 72
tattoo Tätowierung 12
team Team, Mannschaft, Gruppe 34
technical technisch 26
technician Techniker / in 8
temperature Temperatur 51
tense Zeit, Zeitform 87
terrible furchtbar, fürchterlich 13
to test testen, ausprobieren 16
to text sb eine SMS / Kurznachricht schicken 47
text SMS 64
text messaging Versenden von SMS 65
than *(nach Komparativ:)* als 48
thanks a lot vielen Dank 16
thanks very much vielen Dank 10
theory Theorie 46
ticket Fahrschein 16
tie Krawatte 74
tip Tipp, Hinweis 15

to (Uhrzeit:) vor 14
toaster Toaster 96
toilet Toilette 97
toll free *(AE:)* gebührenfrei 25
top Oberteil 58
top man *etwa:* Spitzenmann 36
topic Thema 29
traffic lights Ampel 76
to train eine Ausbildung machen 20
to train sb jdn ausbilden 82
trainers Turnschuhe 16
to translate übersetzen 64
transmitter Sender 65
to transport transportieren, befördern 70
trick Trick, Kniff 15
truck *(AE:)* Lkw, Lastwagen 23
truck driver *(AE:)* Lastwagenfahrer / in, Fernfahrer / in 23
to turn off ausschalten 75
twice zweimal 17
twins Zwillinge 9
typical typisch, normal 40

U

unattended unbeaufsichtigt 71
uncle Onkel 26
underground U-Bahn 52
unemployed arbeitslos 82
unfortunately unglücklicherweise, leider 65
unhappy unzufrieden, unglücklich 72
unit Lektion 20
unsuccessful erfolglos 82
user Nutzer / in 57

V

vacation *(AE:)* Ferien 93
to veg herumhängen 45
vegetables Gemüse 16
vehicle Fahrzeug 34
verb Verb 17
village Dorf 58
visit Besuch 20
visitor Besucher / in 41

vocational college Berufsbildende Schule 15
volt Volt 71
volunteer Freiwillige / r 98

W

wages Lohn 95
waiter Kellner 16
walk Spaziergang, Rundgang 29
walking Wandern, Spazierengehen 10
wall bracket Wandhalterung 96
wall clock Wanduhr 96
wardrobe Kleiderschrank 97
washbasin Waschbecken 97
washing machine Waschmaschine 10
Watch out! Achtung! Vorsicht! 37
to watch TV fernsehen 19
way Weg, Art (und Weise) 62
to weigh wiegen 65
weight Gewicht 39
to welcome wilkommen heißen, begrüßen 17
western westlich, West- 37
wet nass, feucht 71
What about you? Und du? 7
What time is it? Wie spät ist es? Wieviel Uhr ist es? 14
wheel Rad 52
whether ob 25
to work out trainieren 15
work placement Praktikum 75
worker Arbeiter / in 8
workplace Arbeitsplatz 72
workshop Werkstatt 34
world champion Weltmeister / in 88
world championship Weltmeisterschaft 88
worldwide auf der ganzen Welt, weltweit 20

Y

yeah ja 16
You're welcome. Bitte. Gern geschehen. 10
youth Jugend 16
youth hostel Jugendherberge 16

Entry page 12 – Quiz key

Mats Hummels
1 T
2 F (he plays for Germany and Borussia Dortmund)
3 T
4 F (he does have a younger brother who is a footballer but his name is Jonas Hummels)
5 T

Lady Gaga
6 b
7 c
8 a
9 a

Robert Pattinson
10 T
11 F (he is from London, England)
12 F (his middle names are Douglas Thomas)
13 T
14 T

Factfile: The English-speaking world

	United Kingdom (UK)	The United States of America (USA)	Canada	Australia	New Zealand
Size (sq. km.)	242,514	9.8 million	9.9 million	7.7 million	270,534
Highest mountain	Ben Nevis (Scotland) 1,343m	Mount McKinley (Alaska) 6,194m	Mount Logan 5,959m	Mount Kosciuszko 2,229m	Mount Cook 3,754m
Capital/largest city	London/London	Washington DC/New York	Ottawa/Toronto	Canberra/Sydney	Wellington/Auckland
Population	60 million (English 84%, Scottish 8%, Welsh 5%, Northern Irish 3%)	300 million (white 67%, black 13%, Hispanic 14%, Asian 4%, Native American 1%)	32 million (81% English-speaking, 19% French-speaking)	21 million (2% Aborigines)	4.1 million (8% Maori)
Top people and parliament	Queen, Prime Minister, *House of Commons, House of Lords*	President, *House of Representatives, Senate*	Governor General, Prime Minister, *House of Commons, Senate*	Governor General, Prime Minister, *House of Representatives, Senate*	Governor General, Prime Minister, *House of Representatives*
Important exports	banking, insurance, manufactured goods, chemicals, food	computers, electrical goods, vehicles, food, military equipment, planes	machinery, metals, plastics, wood products, agricultural and fish products	metals, wool, live animals, transport machinery	wool, food and dairy products, wood and paper
Average income (year)	€26,000	€32,000	€25,000	€26,000	€22,000
Money	pound sterling (£)	US dollar ($)	Canadian dollar (C$)	Australian dollar (A$)	New Zealand dollar (NZ$)
Popular sports	football, cricket, rugby	American football, baseball	ice hockey	cricket, rugby	rugby, sailing
Internet domain	.uk	.us	.ca	.au	.nz
International dialling code	+44	+1	+1	+61	+64
Famous people	William Shakespeare, the Queen, David Beckham, Prince William, J.K. Rowling (author of *Harry Potter*)	George Washington (first president), Henry Ford (first mass-produced cars), Neil Armstrong (first man on the moon), lots of film stars!	Avril Lavigne, Alanis Morissette, Keanu Reeves, James Naismith (invented basketball)	Mel Gibson, Nicole Kidman, Kylie Minogue, Rupert Murdoch (started Sky TV)	Peter Jackson (director of *Lord Of The Rings*), Russell Crowe, A.J. Hackett (invented bungee jumping)

Bildquellennachweis

4.1 Getty Images (Digital Vision/Michael Blann), München; **4.2** iStockphoto (Aldo Murillo), Calgary, Alberta; **4.3** Fotolia.com (Victoria Andreas), New York; **4.4** Fotolia.com (Alexander Raths), New York; **4.5** Getty Images (Bloomberg), München; **5.1** iStockphoto (Daniel Laflor), Calgary, Alberta; **5.2** JupiterImages photos.com (Photos.com), Tucson, AZ; **5.3** Thinkstock, (Stokkete/iStock), München; **5.4** iStockphoto (Kyoshino), Calgary, Alberta; **5.5** shutterstock (George Dolgikh), New York, NY; **6.1** Getty Images (Digital Vision/Michael Blann), München; **6.2** shutterstock (Mat Hayward), New York, NY; **8.1** Thinkstock (Hemera), München; **8.2** Fotolia.com (Goodluz), New York; **8.3** JupiterImages photos.com (photos.com), Tucson, AZ; **8.4** shutterstock (Tyler Olson), New York, NY; **8.5** shutterstock (Wavebreakmedia), New York, NY; **9.1** shutterstock (Andrey Arkusha), New York, NY; **9.2** shutterstock (Lisa F. Young), New York, NY; **9.3** iStockphoto (Linda Kloosterhof), Calgary, Alberta; **9.4** Fotolia.com (Maya Kruchancova), New York; **10.1** iStockphoto (Sun Chan), Calgary, Alberta; **10.2** PantherMedia GmbH (Djem), München; **11** shutterstock (Vlad G), New York, NY; **12.1** Imago (Karina Hessland), Berlin; **12.2** shutterstock (Joe Seer), New York, NY; **12.3** dreamstime.com (Featureflash), Brentwood, TN; **14.1** iStockphoto (Klaas Lingbeek-van Kranen), Calgary, Alberta; **14.2** Thinkstock (Eyecandy Images), München; **15** Fotolia.com (Goodluz), New York; **17** Thinkstock (iStockphoto), München; **18** Thinkstock (Hemera), München; **20.1** iStockphoto (Aldo Murillo), Calgary, Alberta; **20.2** iStockphoto (Kristaps Dislers), Calgary, Alberta; **22** iStockphoto (Aldo Murillo), Calgary, Alberta; **23.1** iStockphoto (Aldo Murillo), Calgary, Alberta; **23.2** shutterstock (Rudy Balasko), New York, NY; **24** shutterstock (Piotr Marcinski), New York, NY; **25** shutterstock (Auremar), New York, NY; **28** iStockphoto (Kirby Hamilton), Calgary, Alberta; **29** Klett-Archiv, Stuttgart; **31** BigStockPhoto.com (Corepics), Davis, CA; **32.1** Fotolia.com (Victoria Andreas), New York; **32.2** iStockphoto (Ranplett), Calgary, Alberta; **34** Fotolia.com (Tyler Olson), New York; **35.1** shutterstock (Nikkytok), New York, NY; **35.2** iStockphoto (BlueOrange Studio), Calgary, Alberta; **35.3** shutterstock (Monkey Business Images), New York, NY; **35.4** iStockphoto (Anne-Louise Quarfoth), Calgary, Alberta; **40** iStockphoto (Susanna Fieramosca Naranjo), Calgary, Alberta; **41** HarperCollins, London-Hammersmith; **42** Fotolia.com (Filipemfrazao), New York; **43.1** iStockphoto (Kristian Septimius Krogh), Calgary, Alberta; **43.2** dreamstime.com (Michel Bussieres), Brentwood, TN; **44.1**; **44.3** Fotolia.com (Alexander Raths), New York; **44.2** iStockphoto (Dutchicon), Calgary, Alberta; **44.4** shutterstock (Subbotina Anna), New York, NY; **44.5** dreamstime.com (Wellphotos), Brentwood, TN; **45.1** shutterstock (Cynthia Farmer), New York, NY; **45.2** Fotolia.com, New York; **45.3** shutterstock (Scyther5), New York, NY; **45.4** Fotolia.com (quipu), New York; **46.1** Fotolia.com (yanlev), New York; **46.2** Fotolia.com (Springfield Galler), New York; **46.3** Fotolia.com (Tigger11th), New York; **46.4** Thinkstock (Big Cheese Photo), München; **46.5** shutterstock (Olena Zaskochenko), New York, NY; **46.6** Fotolia.com (Roman Milert), New York; **47** Fotolia.com (Alexander Raths), New York; **48** iStockphoto (Kgelati1), Calgary, Alberta; **49.1** Thinkstock (Steve Vanhorn/iStock), München; **49.2** Fotolia.com (Olyina), New York; **49.3** Thinkstock (Dominik Heyer/iStock), München; **49.4** Thinkstock (Svetlana Turilova/iStock), München; **49.5** iStockphoto (Cclickclick), Calgary, Alberta; **49.6** Thinkstock (Barbara DudziÂska/iStock), München; **50** shutterstock (Goodluz), New York, NY; **51** Fotolia.com (Anatoliy Lukich), New York; **52.1** shutterstock (Kamira), New York, NY; **52.2** iStockphoto (Lorraine Boogich), Calgary, Alberta; **53.1** iStockphoto (Carrollphoto), Calgary, Alberta; **53.2** iStockphoto (Microgen), Calgary, Alberta; **53.3** Thinkstock (LuminaStock/iStock), München; **53.4** shutterstock (Markus Kaemmerer), New York, NY; **53.5** Florian Foest, Berlin; **55** iStockphoto (Nyul), Calgary, Alberta; **56.1** Getty Images (Bloomberg), München; **56.2** shutterstock (AHMAD FAIZAL YAHYA), New York, NY; **58.1** iStockphoto (Cloki), Calgary, Alberta; **58.2** adidas AG, Herzogenaurach; **58.3** iStockphoto (Eva Serrabassa), Calgary, Alberta; **60** Coca Cola; **60.1** iStockphoto (Abel Mitja Varela), Calgary, Alberta; **60.2** Interfoto (Sammlung Rauch), München; **60.3** Interfoto, München; **60.4** Picture-Alliance (The Coca Cola Company), Frankfurt; **60.5** akg-images, Berlin; **60.6** iStockphoto (Robtek), Calgary, Alberta; **60.8** Mauritius Images (Alamy), Mittenwald; **61.1** Corbis (Bettmann), Düsseldorf; **61.2** dreamstime.com (Mark Williamson), Brentwood, TN; **63** iStockphoto (Kin Yan Chew), Calgary, Alberta; **64** shutterstock (Petrenko Andriy), New York, NY; **65** Picture-Alliance (EPA/PRINCE OF ASTURIAS FOUNDATION/HO), Frankfurt; **65** Klett-Archiv, Stuttgart; **67.1** shutterstock (Andresr), New York, NY; **67.2** shutterstock (Monticello), New York, NY; **68.1** Fotolia.com (.shock), New York; **68.2** iStockphoto (Daniel Laflor), Calgary, Alberta; **68.3** Thinkstock (Brand X Pictures), München; **68.4** shutterstock (CandyBox Images), New York, NY; **70** shutterstock (Oriontrail), New York, NY; **72** shutterstock (Wavebreakmedia), New York, NY; **75** Thinkstock (Digital Vision.), München; **76.1**; **76.2**; **76.3**; **76.7**; **76.8** URW, Hamburg; **76.4** iStockphoto (Compucow), Calgary, Alberta; **77.1** shutterstock (lightpoet), New York, NY; **77.2** HarperCollins, London-Hammersmith; **79.1** iStockphoto (Piskel), Calgary, Alberta; **79.2** iStockphoto (Jophil), Calgary, Alberta; **80.1** JupiterImages photos.com (Photos.com), Tucson, AZ; **80.2** iStockphoto (Michal Koziarski), Calgary, Alberta; **82.1** Picture-Alliance (UPPA/Photoshot), Frankfurt; **82.2** Alamy Images (Allstar Picture Library), Abingdon, Oxon; **84.1** Fotolia.com (Robert Neumann), New York; **84.2** Thinkstock (iStockphoto), München; **84.3** shutterstock (Michael Jung), New York, NY; **85.1** iStockphoto (Jallfree), Calgary, Alberta; **87** shutterstock (Supri Suharjoto), New York, NY; **88** Thinkstock (Jupiterimages), München; **89** HarperCollins, London-Hammersmith; **90.1** iStockphoto (Lise Gagne), Calgary, Alberta; **92.1** Thinkstock (Stokkete/iStock), München; **92.2** Thinkstock

(Jupiterimages/Stockbyte), München; **94.1** iStockphoto (Teun van den Dries), Calgary, Alberta; **94.2** shutterstock (Phase4Studios), New York, NY; **95** iStockphoto (Milenko Bokan), Calgary, Alberta; **96** iStockphoto (Bortonia), Calgary, Alberta; **96** shutterstock (Benchart), New York, NY; **96** Fotolia.com (Pilarts), New York; **96** iStockphoto (Geopaul), Calgary, Alberta; **96** Fotolia.com (Nicemonkey), New York; **96** Thinkstock (istock/Colematt), München; **96** shutterstock (Wayne Marques), New York, NY; **96** shutterstock (Dan Nurgitz), New York, NY; **96** Thinkstock (iStock/Miro Kovacevic), München; **96** Thinkstock (iStock/Dmitry Merkushin), München; **96** shutterstock (Peter Hermes Furian), New York, NY; **96** Fotolia.com (Jermvut Kitchaichank), New York; **96** Thinkstock (iStock/Janfilip), München; **96** shutterstock (Colorlife), New York, NY; **96.1** Thinkstock (Oticki/iStock), München; **97** shutterstock (Radu Bercan), New York, NY; **97** shutterstock (paranormal), New York, NY; **98.1** Fotolia.com (Floki Fotos), New York; **98.2** Fotolia.com (Jolopes), New York; **98.3** iStockphoto (Christopher Futcher), Calgary, Alberta; **99** Fotolia.com (CandyBox Images), New York; **101** Klett-Archiv, Stuttgart; **103** iStockphoto (Michael Jung), Calgary, Alberta; **104** iStockphoto (Kyoshino), Calgary, Alberta; **105** iStockphoto (Milenko Bokan), Calgary, Alberta; **106** Thinkstock (William87), München; **108** iStockphoto (Kupicoo), Calgary, Alberta; **109** iStockphoto (Image Source), Calgary, Alberta; **110** Thinkstock (Wavebreak Media), München; **112.1** shutterstock (Yuri Arcurs), New York, NY; **112.2** iStockphoto (Troels Graugaard), Calgary, Alberta; **112.3** iStockphoto (Tyler Olson), Calgary, Alberta; **114.1** iStockphoto (Thp73), Calgary, Alberta; **114.2** iStockphoto (Josef Mohyla), Calgary, Alberta; **114.3** Thinkstock (Purestock), München; **115.1** shutterstock (Wally Stemberger), New York, NY; **115.2** Thinkstock (iStockphoto), München; **116** iStockphoto (Mark Bowden), Calgary, Alberta; **118** shutterstock (George Dolgikh), New York, NY; **129** Stockbyte, Tralee, County Kerry; **COVER** Thinkstock (Eyecandy Images), München

Sollte es in einem Einzelfall nicht gelungen sein, den korrekten Rechteinhaber ausfindig zu machen, so werden berechtigte Ansprüche selbstverständlich im Rahmen der üblichen Regelungen abgegolten.